PENGUIN HANDBOOKS

LYN ST. JAMES'S
CAR OWNER'S MANUAL FOR WOMEN

Lyn St. James entered her first race on a dare at age 17. Since then, she has become one of the top women drivers in the world, racing from Daytona, Florida, to Sears Point, California. A native of Willoughby, Ohio, she earned a teaching certificate at the St. Louis Institute of Music, with the intention of pursuing her primary interest: classical piano. She taught piano for several years.

In addition to pursuing her racing career, she travels extensively throughout North America as principal spokeswoman for Ford Motor Company's marketing program for women, conducting clinics on ''car owning made easy.'' She appears frequently on radio and television. Ms. St. James also is owner and president of Autodyne, a wholesale automotive parts distributorship in Dania, Florida.

When not on the road, she lives in Fort Lauderdale, Florida.

Lyn St. James's Car Owner's Manual for Women

by Lyn St. James

A Tilden Press Book

PENGUIN BOOKS

Penguin Books Ltd, Harmondsworth,
Middlesex, England
Penguin Books, 40 West 23rd Street,
New York, New York 10010, U.S.A.
Penguin Books Australia Ltd, Ringwood,
Victoria, Australia
Penguin Books Canada Limited, 2801 John Street,
Markham, Ontario, Canada L3R 1B4
Penguin Books (N.Z.) Ltd , 182-190 Wairau Road,
Auckland 10, New Zealand

First published 1984

Printed in the United States of America by
Command Web Offset Inc., Secaucus, New Jersey

Book design by Judith Connelly
Illustrations by Sai Graphics and Catherine Krebs
A Tilden Press Book

To my mother,
who taught me how to drive and take care of
the family car, and who always encouraged
me to do what I felt was best. She's a special lady.

Contents

Acknowledgments

A number of individuals and companies supplied inspiration, information, and assistance in helping me put this book together. Their efforts were invaluable and are greatly appreciated. I'd particularly like to thank Ford Motor Company, Art Schultz, Joel Makower, Kathryn Court, Barbara Jaekle, and Don Courtney.

Introduction

Buying and owning a car is a major commitment of time and money. It probably is your second biggest commitment, after your home.

This book is designed to make that commitment a satisfying one by increasing your knowledge and appreciation of cars. In nontechnical terms, you'll learn what you should know about buying, owning, operating, and selling an automobile. I call it "demystifying" the automobile.

As cars become more sophisticated, and as repair and maintenance costs increase, it is more important than ever to be well informed about the world of automobiles. The more you know, the more satisfied you will be—initially and throughout your car's lifetime.

Today, women have tremendous clout in the automotive marketplace. Of the $75 billion spent annually on new cars, $35 billion (about 45 percent) is spent by women. Yet most women are uncomfortable with cars, both financially and mechanically. Women often lack technical knowledge and confidence when dealing with the "experts" like dealers and mechanics. But this lack of confidence is due more to a lack of exposure and experience than to a lack of ability.

We command economic clout, so we should equip ourselves with the knowledge to use it.

The auto industry has recognized our clout and is beginning to respond to our needs and desires. Automobile companies and dealers are anxious to please us because they are anxious for our business. Contrary to conventional wisdom, we are concerned with the practical and functional aspects of cars, not just the color and design. Because we are excellent shoppers, we are more likely to seek sound information about safety, reliability, and economy. And we are very active in shopping competitively before we buy.

Why, then, are cars still so frightening? Because we lack a basic working knowledge of the world of cars.

Long before I ever dreamed of becoming a race-car driver, I had a fascination with cars. I had to depend on the family car to get me back and forth from school and work. In a way, I was lucky: My mother made me learn the basic maintenance routines. If I didn't keep checking the oil, the tire pressure, the radiator, and several other things, I simply couldn't use the car. Later, I had a part-time summer job at a local gas station, where I learned more about keeping the family car in tiptop shape.

After high-school graduation, I got my first job, at U.S. Steel's Cleveland District Sales, in downtown Cleveland, about forty miles from home. It was now time to buy my first car!

After long discussions with a local car salesman, a trip to the annual new car show, and more discussions with the salesman, I finally ordered the car I wanted, much to his dismay. You see, after reading brochures and seeking advice, I *knew* what I wanted. And so I special-ordered it: a hot Pontiac 2 + 2, with a four-speed transmission, heavy-duty suspension, special rear-end ratios, and the largest engine available. I'm almost embarrassed to reveal the last part—it was plum with a white interior.

After much arguing with the salesman (and I appreciated his concern), I stuck to my guns. I drove that car for more than two years and was *completely* satisfied with it. I also got a pretty good price when I sold it. It just proves that if you seek enough information and learn what you need to know before buying a car, you can make an intelligent and satisfying choice.

Of course, my interest in cars later developed to a much higher level. I now own an auto parts wholesale distributorship in Dania, Florida. I am a professional race-car driver. And I consult with major corporations in the automotive industry on the woman's point of view in marketing, advertising, and public relations.

Ford Motor Company, an important client, is the first auto maker to implement a major marketing program to target women consumers. When I read a booklet Ford first published in 1911, called *The*

Woman and the Ford, I was fascinated to learn that Ford's interest in women was nothing new. I quote from the booklet:

It's a woman's day. Her own is coming home to her—her "ownest own." She shares the responsibilities—and demands the opportunities and pleasures of the new order. No longer a "shut in," she reaches for an ever wider sphere of action—that she may be more the woman. And in this happy change the automobile is playing no small part. It has broadened her horizon—increased her pleasures—given new vigor to her body—made neighbors of far away friends—and multiplied tremendously her range of activity. It is a real weapon in the changing order.

More than seven decades later, those words still ring true. And now that cars have "broadened our horizons," it's time to broaden our horizons about cars.

Come with me through the following pages to the world of cars. It's a world well worth knowing. It's a world that will bring financial rewards and a great deal of personal satisfaction.

Chapter One

How Cars Work

How Cars Work

How well do you know your car and how it works? You turn the key to start the engine. You move the gearshift to go forward or in reverse. You step on the gas pedal to go faster. You turn the steering wheel to change directions and step on the brake to slow down or stop.

What about maintenance? You add gas when you're low and maybe even pump it yourself. You have the oil changed twice a year, the coolant checked before winter, and maybe pay for a tune-up once in a while. Perhaps you add air to your tires when someone tells you they're low. And you drive through a car wash, weather permitting.

Repairs? When the car bounces, you get new shock absorbers. When it rumbles, you have the muffler checked. If you no longer can stop on a dime, you have the brakes checked.

That's a start, but there's much more you can do—if you understand what goes on under the hood, under the car, and behind the dashboard.

It's really not all that complicated. In fact, it may surprise you to know I've already referred to all ten major systems in the car: electrical, fuel, exhaust, transmission, lubrication, cooling, brakes, steering, suspension, and tires and wheels.

When you open the hood, you needn't be intimidated by the confusing maze of hoses, wires, and tubes. Everything has a function, as you'll learn in the pages that follow. A working knowledge of the ten basic systems can go a long way toward keeping your car in shape, talking to a mechanic, and even taking some repairs into your own hands.

The Ten Major Systems

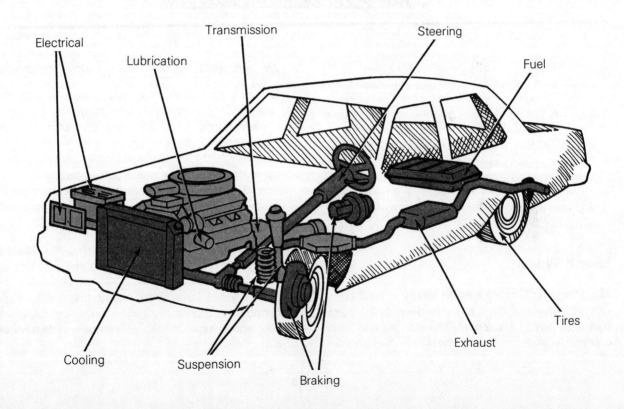

Electrical

Lubrication

Transmission

Steering

Fuel

Cooling

Suspension

Braking

Exhaust

Tires

The Electrical System

If you've ever had a dead battery, you know the importance of the electrical system in getting your car started. That vital role continues once the car gets going. The electricity your car generates and stores in the battery also operates the radio, lights, heater, fuel pump, windshield wipers, horn, and a wide assortment of other gauges and controls.

If your car won't start, or if some of the electrical components aren't working, it may not be the battery's fault. As you'll see, many other parts of the car may be involved.

How It Works

■ When you turn the **ignition key**, you send an electrical charge (stored in the **battery**) to the **starter motor** by way of a **solenoid**. The starter motor spins a gear that engages the **flywheel**, which is bolted to the **crankshaft**, thereby ''turning over'' the engine.

■ Once the engine is working, it becomes the principal power generator. The actual device that performs this function is called the **alternator**. The alternator translates the movement of the engine into electricity, used to recharge the battery (you used up some of the battery's power while starting the car). The alternator not only recharges the battery but sends power to other parts of the car to make your radio, lights, and other components work.

■ When you turned the ignition key, you also sent a twelve-volt charge to your **ignition coil**. The coil actually is a transformer that increases the twelve volts to a powerful 15,000-volt charge that is fed into your **distributor**. This high voltage then is sent directly to your **sparkplugs** through your **rotor** and **distributor cap**.

The Electrical System

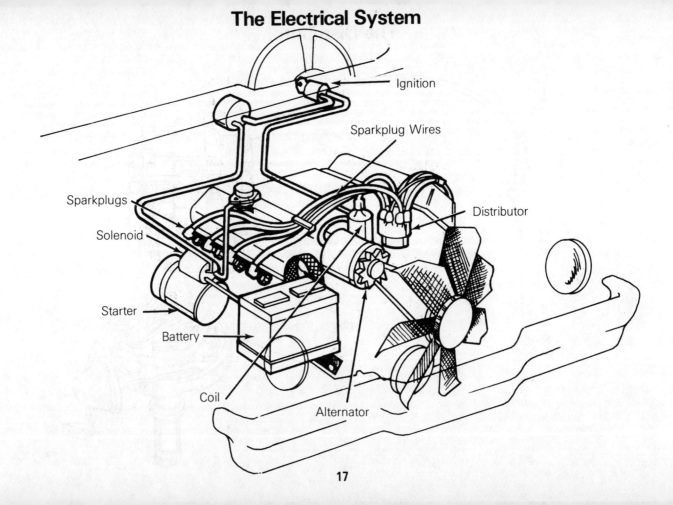

Ignition

Sparkplug Wires

Distributor

Sparkplugs

Solenoid

Starter

Battery

Coil

Alternator

17

The Distributor

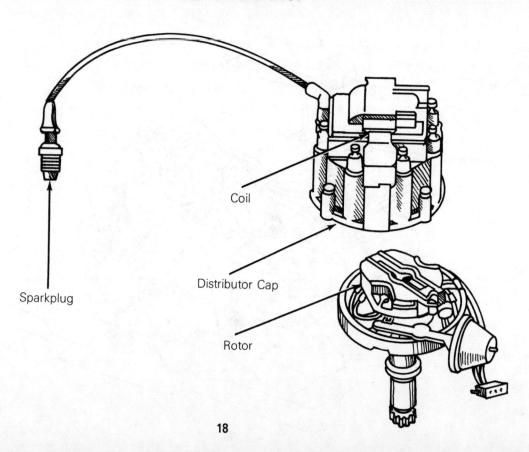

Coil

Sparkplug

Distributor Cap

Rotor

■ As the rotor spins inside your distributor, it touches metal contacts inside the distributor cap thousands of times a minute. This causes a spark across the gap in each sparkplug, which ignites a mixture of gas and air. This explosion forces a **piston** to move, which turns the **crankshaft**, which eventually makes your car run. It all starts with the electrical charge when you turn the ignition key.

There are a few more electrical components you should know about:

■ The **condenser** is a cushion that protects your engine by absorbing excess surges of electricity.

■ **Fuses** and **circuit breakers**, usually located under the dashboard, act as safety valves, too, protecting lights and accessories from surges of excess current.

■ A **voltage regulator** adjusts the amount of electricity produced by the alternator.

What Can Go Wrong

Most electrical parts wear out after a few years. For example:

Battery cables, which connect the battery to the rest of the car, can become corroded or worn, resulting in a poor electrical connection.

The starter and alternator can wear out.

Sparkplugs, points, sparkplug wires, rotors, and the solenoid (which connects the battery to the starter) can become corroded and wear out on a regular basis, resulting in a reduced electrical charge, or no charge at all.

The distributor cap can become worn or cracked, letting in dirt and moisture, which can cause a short circuit. The result is that it is difficult to start the engine or the engine seems to "miss," indicated by an audible gap or "pop" in the engine.

Fuses and circuit breakers can blow, causing electrical components—your lights, for example, or your horn or radio—to become inoperable.

Lights can fail to operate, because of a burned-out bulb, blown fuse, weak battery, defective switch, or out-of-adjustment voltage regulator. Turn signals may not work properly because of a burned-out flasher unit—a little metal box that plugs in under the dashboard.

Other accessories, including the windshield wipers, windshield washer, and horn, may fail to operate because of a defective switch, short circuit, blown fuse, or burned-out motor.

What You Should Do

Battery. If you keep it clean, filled with water, and fully charged, a good battery will last for two or three years, or about 40,000 miles or more. If you have a ''maintenance-free,'' sealed battery, you need not check the fluid level. If your battery isn't

Don't smoke when working around gasoline or cleaning solvents, or when the battery is being charged. (As the battery is being charged, it gives off explosive hydrogen gas.)

''maintenance-free,'' check the fluid level monthly; add distilled water to each cell that is low, and then run your car for a half hour to recharge.

Your battery has two terminal posts, one ''positive'' and one ''negative.'' They have a tendency to build up a layer of corrosion, which can weaken your electrical system. Clean the posts occasionally with a paste of baking soda and water. Let it foam and then rinse with water. Do not allow the mixture to get into the battery cells. After cleaning, apply a thin film of petroleum jelly or a commercial spray to prevent corrosion.

If your car seems hard to start, the problem may be a weak battery. A service-station mechanic can test your battery with a machine that tells whether it needs recharging; another machine can recharge your battery.

Battery cables, one attached to each terminal post, also must be kept free of corrosion and excessive dirt and must be connected securely to the battery. After cleaning the terminals, make sure the bolts holding the cables are tight.

The distributor cap, designed to insulate the rotor and points, may need to be replaced about once a year as part of a tune-up.

Blown fuses or circuit breakers can easily be replaced (fuses) or turned back on (circuit breakers), but the cause should be traced to prevent further damage, or even fire.

Lights, and the plastic or glass lens covers that protect them, may need to be replaced if broken or burned out.

Sparkplugs need to be adjusted, cleaned, or replaced about once a year as part of a tune-up.

The Fuel System

The purpose of the fuel system is very simple: to get fuel from the gas tank to the engine. But a car can't run on plain gas as it comes out of the pump. This liquid fuel must be mixed with air to form a fine mist, which is compressed and exploded, creating the "internal combustion" that makes a car go from here to there.

The efficiency of a car—how many miles you get per gallon—is based partially on the condition of your fuel system. If it's not up to par, you'll simply waste gas and pollute the air.

How It Works

■ The **fuel pump** brings fuel from the **gas tank** through the fuel line. Along the way, it passes through a **fuel filter**, which removes impurities that can clog the fuel line and impair engine performance.

■ When the fuel reaches the **carburetor**, it is mixed with air to create the optimal fuel/air mixture. A valve called a **choke** enriches the mixture when the engine is cold, making the car easier to start. Most newer cars are equipped with an automatic choke.

■ The air portion of the fuel/air mixture flows through an **air filter**, which keeps abrasive dust from the carburetor and engine. (Your engine, by the way, consumes 10,000 times more air than fuel.)

■ The carburetor "feeds" the engine the right amount of gas and air it needs to operate.

■ A **PCV** (for "positive crankcase ventilation") valve recycles unburned gases by sending them back into the engine, where they are safely and efficiently burned.

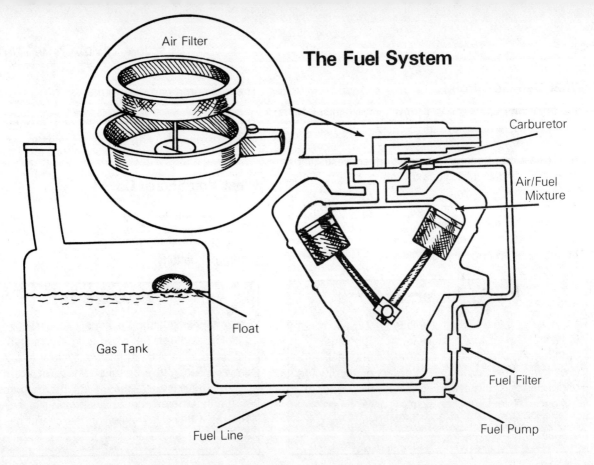

The Fuel System

Air Filter

Carburetor

Air/Fuel Mixture

Float

Gas Tank

Fuel Filter

Fuel Line

Fuel Pump

Fuel

What Can Go Wrong

The carburetor can wear out from age or neglect, requiring repair, rebuild, or replacement.

The air filter can become dirty or clogged, restricting the air flow and reducing gas mileage.

The fuel filter can become clogged, restricting the flow of fuel to the carburetor.

The fuel lines, pump, and gas tank can develop leaks.

The fuel pump can wear out.

The PCV valve can become clogged, restricting its functions and allowing polluting fumes to escape.

What You Should Do

Have your engine tuned at least once a year or every 12,000 miles (see page 78 for more on tune-ups) or check your owner's manual for the manufacturer's recommendations.

Fuel Injection

Many newer cars have fuel injection, a system that "injects" the air-fuel mixture into each engine cylinder, eliminating the need for a carburetor. Fuel injection systems produce better fuel economy and performance and make the engine more responsive. But because fuel injection systems are more sophisticated, they are more difficult and expensive to maintain.

Diesel Engines

Diesel engines usually are more fuel-efficient than gasoline engines, but often are hard to start and produce noise and exhaust smells not found with gas engines. While diesel engines also are more expensive to purchase, they give better fuel economy, so the initial investment pays off over the long term. The main difference between diesel and gasoline engines is that diesel engines have no sparkplugs.

If you drive in a polluted or dusty area, change the air filter every six months.

If you often drive with an almost-empty fuel tank, replace your fuel filter twice a year. An empty tank allows more impurities to get into the fuel—and into the fuel line. If you use "gasohol" (a gasoline and alcohol mixture available at some service stations), change the fuel filter when you first switch, then go back to normal change schedules.

Avoid driving with your fuel tank less than one-quarter full. Don't rely on your "reserve" tank.

Fuel

The Exhaust System

Your car produces a lot of poisonous fumes, resulting from the "internal combustion" and intense heat that goes on inside your engine when you drive. In addition, your engine creates a lot of loud noises, resulting from the "explosions" that take place thousands of times a minute as each sparkplug ignites a pressurized mixture of air and fuel.

The role of the exhaust system is to remove the fumes safely from the car, to minimize the amount of pollution, and to reduce the loud engine sounds into a smooth, soft purr.

How It Works

■ As the air/fuel/sparkplug "explosions" take place inside each cylinder of the engine, the resulting fumes are collected in an **exhaust manifold** and sent through an **exhaust pipe** underneath the car.

■ On most newer cars, the exhaust pipe routes the fumes through a **catalytic converter**, which extracts the unburned hydrocarbons (a major source of air pollution).

■ As the fumes leave the catalytic converter, they pass through a **muffler**, which contains a series of chambers to absorb the noise of the explosions blasting from the engine.

■ Finally, the fumes pass through the **tailpipe** and out into the air.

The Exhaust System

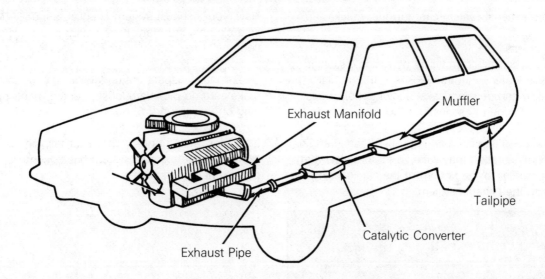

Exhaust Manifold

Muffler

Exhaust Pipe

Catalytic Converter

Tailpipe

What Can Go Wrong

The entire exhaust system can corrode, crack, and develop leaks.

The muffler can fail from inside corrosion, resulting from ''acid water'' that condenses in the muffler. The muffler also can develop leaks, allowing poisonous carbon monoxide to escape into the car.

Backfiring (resulting from an improperly tuned engine) and general vibration may weaken the brackets that hold the muffler to the bottom of the car, causing damage to the exhaust system.

When pumping your own gas, take your keys and credit card or cash—but not your purse—with you and lock your car. Your possessions will be safe and you'll have free use of your hands.

What You Should Do

Have your exhaust system checked annually. Make sure clamps and brackets are snug and seals are tight.

Occasionally inspect the underside of your car to make sure no pipes are loose, dented, bent, or dragging on the ground.

Listen for rattling noises from your tailpipe—a danger signal that the exhaust system has become deteriorated or detached.

The Transmission System

This is one of the most complex systems in your car — and one of the most important. The transmission allows your car to move forward and in reverse at different speeds. Simply put, the transmission "transmits" the power of the engine to the wheels via a series of gears and pumps. The fuel efficiency of your car is related directly to your transmission system.

You probably already know the two basic types of transmissions: manual and automatic. With manual transmissions, you decide when to change gears and provide some of the manual labor required. With automatic transmissions, the car makes most of the gear-changing decisions for you—and provides most of the labor to get the job done.

The transmission is the part of the car most people neglect, say professional mechanics. But that neglect can be costly, leading to transmission overhauls or even replacement. A bit of simple preventive maintenance can save you a lot of money in the long run.

How It Works

■ When you step on the gas, you cause the **crankshaft** to turn. The more gas you give, the faster the crankshaft turns.

■ At the end of the crankshaft is a **flywheel**, a round plate that spins at the same speed as the crankshaft.

■ In manual transmission cars, the flywheel is connected to a **clutch**, which connects or disconnects the power from the engine to the rest of the **drive train**. The **transmission gears** properly match the engine's power with the driving speed, and the **driveshaft** carries that power through the **differential** to the driving wheels (the rear wheels, unless it's a

The Transmission System

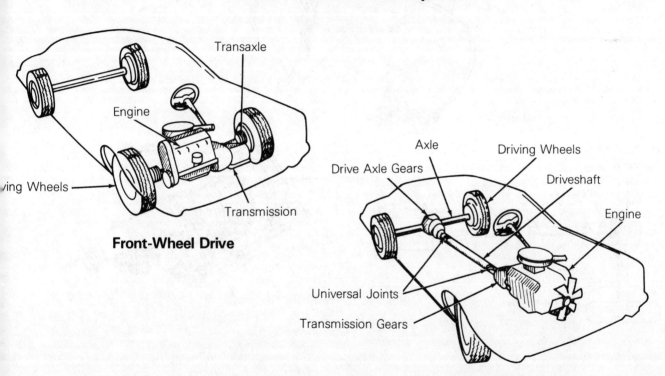

Transaxle

Engine

ving Wheels

Transmission

Front-Wheel Drive

Axle

Driving Wheels

Drive Axle Gears

Driveshaft

Engine

Universal Joints

Transmission Gears

Rear-Wheel Drive

The Transmission System

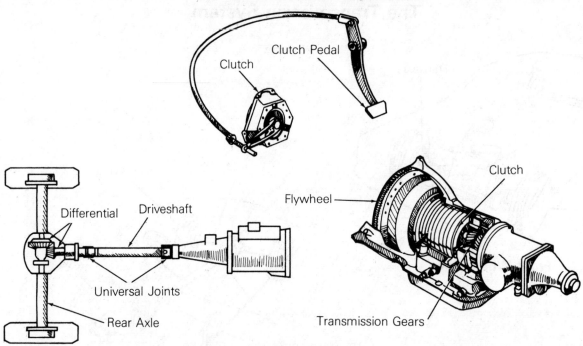

Clutch

Clutch Pedal

Clutch

Flywheel

Differential

Driveshaft

Universal Joints

Rear Axle

Transmission Gears

front-wheel-drive car). The drive shaft is connected by **U-joints** (also called ''universal joints'') to the transmission at one end and to the differential at the other end.

■ In automatic transmission cars, **automatic transmission fluid (ATF)**, a very thin oil, flows through a series of hydraulic pumps and valves to allow automatic shifting of gears. It also lubricates and cools the system. ATF flows through an **ATF filter**, which keeps it free of contaminants that can harm the transmission system.

■ The **modulator**, a small vacuum device, monitors the load on the engine to insure smooth shifting of the gears according to driving speed and other factors.

What Can Go Wrong

Seals in the transmission housing can wear, causing the automatic transmission fluid to leak.

Automatic transmission fluid, through normal wear, can lose its lubricating capabilities. As a result, your gears won't shift easily and can wear out.

The clutch can become out of adjustment. You'll notice this because the clutch will ''slip'' or ''grab.''

The U-joints in the driveshaft can wear out.

The transmission gears can become worn from age or abuse.

If you want to find out whether your car has ever been recalled, call the government's automobile safety hotline: 800-424-9393 (in Washington, D.C., 426-0123). If your car model has been recalled, you may be entitled to free repairs.

Transmission

What You Should Do

Check the level of the automatic transmission fluid regularly. The dipstick usually is located at the rear of the engine block. Before you check the ATF level, warm the engine up; keep the engine running while you check the level. Add ATF in small increments. Most service stations carry open cans.

When changing the transmission fluid, always change the automatic transmission filter too.

Have the clutch adjusted periodically to minimize wear and tear on the transmission gears.

Inspect the tube or hose that connects the modulator to the engine, and replace it if it is defective.

The Lubrication System

In an engine, dozens of metal parts move at high speeds under intense temperatures—more than 4,000 degrees Fahrenheit. Without lubrication, they would grind together and wear away. Oil keeps them moving smoothly and efficiently and, properly changed, gives your car a long, happy life. It is the lifeblood of your car.

In fact, changing your oil at proper intervals is probably the most important maintenance task you can perform. If you choose oil carefully—using only the class and viscosity (thickness) recommended in your owner's manual—you will add years to your car's life.

How It Works

■ At the base of your car's engine is a **crankcase** that holds the **crankshaft, oil pan, oil pump,** and **engine oil**.

■ The oil pump sends the oil from the crankcase to the various moving parts of the engine. The oil lubricates, seals, and cools the engine parts. Its additives help keep the engine clean.

■ The oil is cleaned as it travels through an **oil filter**.

What Can Go Wrong

The oil, if not properly maintained, can get dirty and thick.

Leaks can develop in the lubrication system.

The oil pump and filter can get clogged or wear out.

The Lubrication System

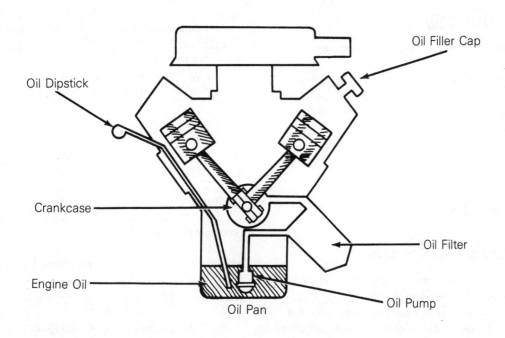

Oil Filler Cap

Oil Dipstick

Crankcase

Oil Filter

Engine Oil

Oil Pump

Oil Pan

Lubrication

What You Should Do

Check the engine oil level weekly (see below). The dipstick is clearly marked to help you determine when the oil level is low. Add oil only when the level is down one or more quarts, and always add one full quart at a time. Overfilling can cause unnecessary oil leaks.

Change oil every six months or 7,500 miles (or whatever the owner's manual recommends).

Change the oil filter every time you change oil and make sure it is tightly fitted.

How to Check Your Car's Oil

To check your car's oil, make sure the car is parked on a flat surface with the engine warmed up but turned off. Remove the dipstick (located under the hood), wipe off the oil at the end, and reinsert it into its slot. Now, remove the dipstick again and read the level.

The dipstick should have at least two marks. The uppermost mark is the ''full'' level, indicating the maximum amount of oil that should be in the engine. The lowest mark indicates the least amount of oil that should be in the engine. Some dipsticks also have a mark in the middle, indicating that you need to add another quart of oil.

If the oil level on the dipstick is at or below the middle of the two marks and you need to add a quart of oil, the procedure is very simple:

■ Remove the oil filler cap, usually located in the center of the engine. But be careful. If the car has been driven in the past two hours, the cap still may be hot.
■ Add one quart of oil, then check the dipstick level again. Do not overfill.
■ Replace the filler cap and tighten.

If you must add oil more than once a month, your engine probably has an oil leak and should be checked by a mechanic.

Checking Your Car's Oil

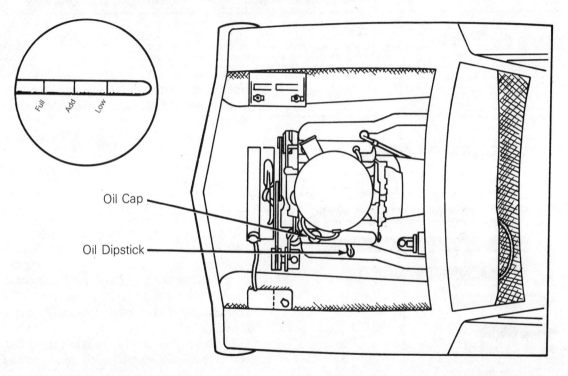

Full Add Low

Oil Cap

Oil Dipstick

Lubrication

39

Choosing the Right Oil

It's important to choose engine oil carefully, using only the class and viscosity recommended in your owner's manual. Many oils today are "multiviscosity," meaning they can be used all year long. Oils that aren't "multiviscosity" get too thick in winter or too thin in summer.

There are seven viscosity grades, each one prefaced by the letters "SAE," which stand for Society of Automotive Engineers, a group that sets industry standards.

A few other things you should know about oil:

■ Oil grades that include a "W" are recommended for cold-weather driving.

■ The lower the number the thinner the oil, meaning the better suited it is for cold-weather use (see chart). An oil graded SAE 10W-30, for example, is appropriate for cars driven in places where winter temperatures plunge to minus-10 degrees Fahrenheit, while an oil graded 5W-30 is appropriate for places where temperatures drop to minus-20 degrees and lower.

Some oils meet only certain car manufacturers' warranty specifications, so it's important to read before you buy.

Sample Oil Grades

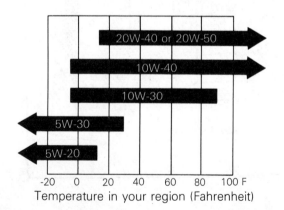

Temperature in your region (Fahrenheit)

The Cooling System

When your car runs, it gets red-hot. When the crankshaft is cranking and the sparkplugs are sparking, the heat generated is sufficient to melt the cast-iron metal parts of the engine in about twenty minutes. But thanks to the cooling system, things stay—well, not exactly *cool*, but cool enough for maximum safety and efficiency. If you let your car overheat, you could be in big trouble.

How It Works

■ The water and antifreeze or coolant you store in your **radiator**, located in front of the engine, is pumped by the **water pump** through the **bottom radiator hose** and is circulated through **water jackets** located around the engine block.

■ The liquid captures the engine's heat, then travels through the **top radiator hose** and, on its way back to the radiator, passes through the **thermostat**, which monitors the temperature. (An automobile's proper operating temperature is about 180 degrees to 205 degrees Fahrenheit.)

■ The **radiator cap** seals in the proper amount of pressure and releases excess pressure.

■ As the engine turns, it also turns a **fan**, which circulates a large volume of air to remove heat from the coolant flowing through the radiator and to provide some direct air to cool the engine.

■ The crankshaft pulley turns a **fan belt,** which drives the water pump, alternator, and fan. (The alternator is part of the electrical system; see page 16.)

The Cooling System

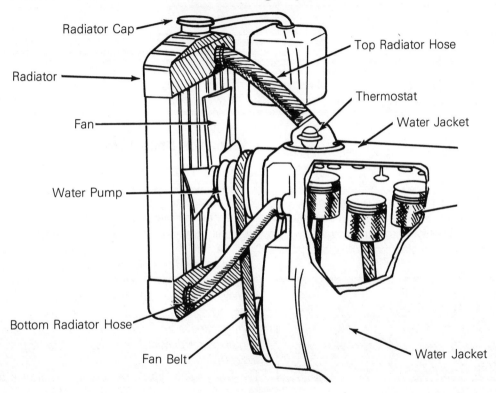

Radiator Cap

Radiator

Fan

Water Pump

Bottom Radiator Hose

Fan Belt

Top Radiator Hose

Thermostat

Water Jacket

Water Jacket

What Can Go Wrong

The fan belt can fray or crack or become too tight or too loose.

Radiator hoses can become brittle, cracked, soft, bulgy, or disconnected.

Your radiator cap can develop a leak. With too little pressure, water will escape.

The radiator—made either of copper or aluminum and consisting of a series of tubes (which direct the flow of water) and fins (which direct the flow of air)—can develop holes or leaks from corrosion or damage.

Don't wear loose clothing while working around the car. You'll protect both you and your car if you remove watches, fancy belt buckles, beads, and the like. Long hair should be hidden under a cap or hat.

The thermostat can malfunction and cause a slow warm-up, increased engine wear, overheating, or engine failure.

The water pump can wear out. It should be replaced if it is leaking or making excessive noise.

What You Should Do

Check the fluid level in the radiator regularly. If you have an overflow container (often called a ''coolant recovery bottle''), it will be marked so you'll know when to add water. If you don't have an overflow container, you'll have to remove the radiator cap to add water.

To remove the radiator cap, be sure to place a cloth on the cap. Turn it slightly to release the pressure slowly. When you remove the cap, tilt it slightly so the opening is pointing away from you. *If the engine is hot, don't—under any circumstances— open the radiator. The pressure and heat can cause severe burns.*

The engine should be running when you add liquid

to the radiator. Fill the radiator right to the top before replacing the cap.

If you live in a cold climate, have your antifreeze/water mixture checked to make certain it is capable of withstanding cold weather. Most service stations will test your antifreeze with a simple little device that tells at what temperature the antifreeze will still work. If the weather in your area will go below that level, you probably need to add more antifreeze.

Check the fan belt periodically and make sure it isn't too loose or too tight. Exactly how loose or tight it should be differs from car to car. Your best bet is to ask a mechanic to show you how tight your car's fan belt should be, so you can check it from time to time.

Check the radiator hoses and hose clamps periodically to make sure they are tight and secure.

Your radiator should be ''flushed'' about once every year or two. This involves removing the water/coolant mixture in the entire cooling system, not just the radiator. You can do this yourself with minimal difficulty using an inexpensive kit available at any auto parts store.

Cooling

The Brake System

The brake system is really very easy to understand. First, it's important to know there are two basic types of braking systems: **drum brakes** and **disc brakes**. With drum brakes, the car stops because **brake shoes** press against **brake drums**, slowing the wheels. With **disc brakes**, wheels are slowed when **brake pads** press against **brake discs**.

How It Works

■ The **brake pedal** is connected to a **master cylinder** under the hood, which is filled with a special **brake fluid**.

■ When you step on the brake pedal, you activate a piston in the master cylinder that forces brake fluid out through a network of steel lines to each of the four wheels.

■ When the brake fluid reaches the wheels, it enters another set of cylinders—called **wheel cylinders** on drum brakes or **brake calipers** on disc brakes.

As the fluid goes through the cylinders, it applies pressure that forces the brake shoes against the brake drums—or the brake pads against the metal discs. The drums and discs, which are part of the wheel assemblies, stop turning and the car comes to a stop.

■ The harder you step on the brake pedal (the more fluid you force through the system), the faster you come to a stop.

■ If your car is equipped with **power brakes**, it is important to remember that they do not stop more quickly, only more easily. Power assist is provided by a **power booster**, located between the brake pedal and the master cylinder, that minimizes pedal effort to make braking easier.

The Brake System

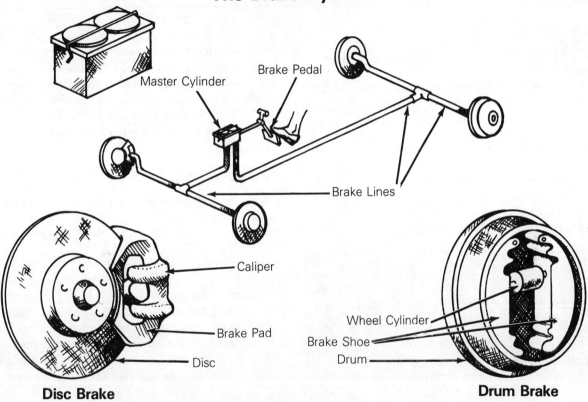

Master Cylinder

Brake Pedal

Brake Lines

Caliper

Brake Pad

Disc

Disc Brake

Wheel Cylinder

Brake Shoe

Drum

Drum Brake

47

What Can Go Wrong

Brake fluid can evaporate and leak, making it more difficult to stop the car; this sometimes is described as a ''spongy'' brake pedal. Brake fluid needs to be replenished periodically. The proper fluid level is ¼ inch from the top of the master cylinder.

If you have to add brake fluid more than twice a year, there probably is a leak in the system. Leaks often occur where the brake lines are sealed together at each wheel and at the master cylinder. You may need to have the brake lines drained and the seals replaced —and, perhaps, the master cylinder rebuilt.

Pay attention to the light that indicates your parking brake is on. This is especially important when going in reverse (as when backing out of a driveway) because the drag of the brake is not as noticeable in reverse as in first gear or ''drive.''

Brake pads and shoes wear out. This happens normally, with the wear and tear of driving. You'll need to replace the pads (on disc brakes) or have the shoes relined (on drum brakes). If pads or shoes are wearing unevenly, there may be more serious problems, usually involving the adjustment of the brake drums or discs. Brake linings should be checked every 10,000 miles.

What You Should Do

Check the brake fluid level once a month, refilling when necessary. Add enough fluid to keep the master cylinder filled to within ¼ inch of the top.

Keep aware of how the brakes feel. If they're spongy—if you don't get immediate response when you step on the pedal—you may have a leaky brake line or need new pads or shoes. (However, the problem may be solved with a few simple adjustments.) If the brakes are pulling the car to one side, there could be a problem with even distribution of brake fluid, or one or more pads or shoes could be wearing unevenly. (It also could be a problem with your tires, but it's smart to check the brakes first.)

Listen to your brakes. If they squeal when you come to a stop, you may need to replace the pads or shoes. If you wait too long—letting the pads or shoes wear out completely—the drums or discs may be damaged, requiring them to be resurfaced or re-placed. That can be an expensive job.

Wheel cylinders should be rebuilt or replaced whenever leaking occurs or brake linings are installed.

Brakes

The Steering System

If you are to drive safely and get good gas mileage, the steering wheel should respond quickly. There should be no movement of the wheel without a corresponding movement of the car. When operating properly, steering should be smooth and easy. The car should hold its course down a straight and level road with little or no correction.

The steering wheel is the one thing in your car with which you are constantly in contact, and it is what puts you in control. It should perform perfectly.

How It Works

■ The **steering wheel** is connected to the **steering column**, which transmits the turning action from the steering wheel to the **steering gear**. The column also houses the wires that control your horn, turn signals, and, in some cars with automatic transmission, the mechanism that sends gear selection to the transmission.

■ The **steering linkage** connects the steering column to the front wheels and moves the wheels to change direction. This linkage consists of a **pitman arm** and **idler arm**. Movable joints in the steering linkage called **ball joints** allow the front wheels to move back and forth like door hinges.

■ If your car is equipped with **power steering**, it has a **power steering pump** that pressurizes the hydraulic **power steering fluid** to help you turn the wheels more easily.

What Can Go Wrong

Improperly aligned wheels can cause your car to pull to one side or the other. (Low air pressure in your tires can cause the same problem.)

The front end of the car may vibrate because of improperly balanced wheels or loose steering linkage.

The Steering System

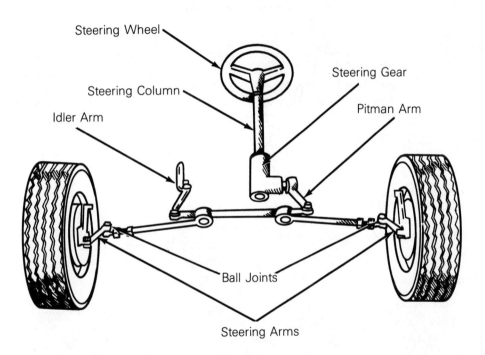

Steering Wheel

Steering Gear

Steering Column

Pitman Arm

Idler Arm

Ball Joints

Steering Arms

If you get your hands greasy when working on your car, some excellent hand cleaners are produced especially for mechanics. These cleaners come as a soft paste and aren't as harsh as cleansers or other solvents. One product, Pro Tek, adds a protective coating, like an invisible glove, before you do messy work.

The steering can get out of adjustment. It will become either too hard or too loose, making driving difficult and unsafe.

What You Should Do

Check your car's power steering fluid regularly. The dipstick is located at the top of the power steering pump under the hood and should have markings that indicate whether you need to add more fluid. When checking, be sure your car is on level ground and bring the engine up to normal operating temperature.

When adding fluid, you can use the same automatic transmission fluid you used in your transmission. Add as much as needed to bring the fluid level up to the ''full'' mark.

If you notice a change in the way your steering wheel responds, you may need to have the steering linkage adjusted.

Most linkage and joints need lubrication. Grease fittings, which act as cushions against wear and friction in the steering linkage, need to be ''lubed'' at the intervals specified in your owner's manual.

Replace the idler arm and pitman arm in your steering linkage when there is evidence of excessive wear.

Keep your car's front end aligned properly to insure exact steering response and proper tire wear. (For details on tires, see page 58.)

The Suspension System

If your car did not have a suspension system, even a short ride to the store could be an uncomfortable experience. You would lose the ability to steer effectively at even the slightest pothole. The suspension system literally "suspends" your car over its four tires, absorbing bumps, potholes, and other rough terrain to give you a smooth, stable ride.

How It Works

■ The **control arms** allow the front wheels to move up and down when going over bumps.

■ The **springs** and **shock absorbers** cushion and absorb shocks between the car and the road. Depending on the car, the suspension system can include **coil springs, leaf springs**, or **torsion bars**. Each of the moving parts of the system has pivot points. Some of these pivots are made of metal and have grease fit-

tings; others are made of rubber.

■ **Stabilizer bars** (sometimes called "anti-sway bars") often are installed on the rear and front axles. They help stabilize the car as it travels over bumps, potholes, and around corners.

■ **Shock absorbers** control the bouncing effect of the springs, reduce vibrations, and resist "body roll" (the car's tendency to lean from side to side). These hydraulic devices smooth out the ride and keep the wheels firmly on the road. There is one shock absorber for each wheel. **MacPherson struts** combine the shock absorber, spring, and "hinges," or ball joints, into a single unit for the front wheels, and sometimes also for the rear wheels. When replacement is necessary, the entire unit must be changed, although sometimes a new shock-absorber section can be inserted.

The Suspension System

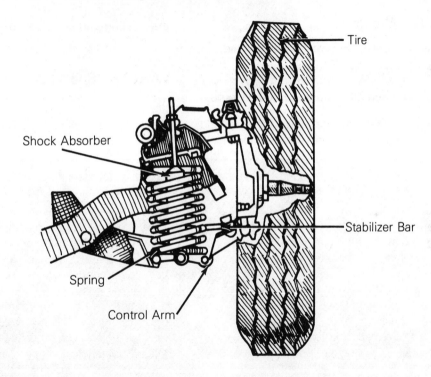

Tire

Shock Absorber

Stabilizer Bar

Spring

Control Arm

What Can Go Wrong

Most suspension problems arise from loss of fluid, broken mountings, and worn inner parts. Worn, inefficient shocks can be identified by severe body sway, front-end dipping when braking, and a bouncing ride.

A badly worn shock can cause irregular tire wear and lead to other mechanical problems, some affecting the steering and vehicle stability, creating a safety hazard.

What You Should Do

Under normal conditions, shock absorbers should be checked about every 15,000 miles, unless they have a lifetime warranty; then they should be checked after

Do You Need New Shocks?

Here's a simple test to check whether your shock absorbers are working correctly. It's called a "bumper test" or "fender test."

■ At each corner of the car, push down on the bumper or fender repeatedly until you have set up a vigorous bouncing motion.

■ Now stop. If the car continues to bounce up and down more than twice, the shocks are not working effectively.

Some brand-new shock absorbers may fail this test, which is a sign they are poorly made and cannot do a very good job of cushioning the car on bumps and turns.

There are several kinds of replacement shock absorbers. You should consider choosing better shocks than those that came with the car. "Heavy-duty" shocks have a longer life expectancy than original-equipment shocks and provide a firmer ride and better car control.

No matter what type you choose, buy shock absorbers designed to fit your make, model, and year car. Never replace just one shock; this can result in dangerous handling of the car. Always replace at least two—both fronts or both rears—or all four.

25,000 miles. High-performance-type shock absorbers with lifetime warranties can last as long as 60,000 miles.

Some of the pivots in the coil or leaf springs require lubrication. Use the lubricant and maintenance intervals prescribed in your owner's manual. Pivots made of rubber should not be lubricated, as grease will cause them to deteriorate. If your car squeaks as it bounces, you may need to tighten or replace rubber pivots. Seek professional advice to determine if a special rubber lubricant can be used to get rid of the noise.

Suspension

Tires and Wheels

Tires are among the most critical items on your car. When you are driving, they are your only contact with Mother Earth. The way in which the tires grip the road affects many things, including comfort, handling, gas mileage, and—most important—the safety of you and your passengers.

Many new cars are equipped with radial tires. If you buy a new car, you should ask for them. If they do not come as "standard equipment," they will be available as options. The additional cost will be recovered many times over in better gas mileage and longer tire life.

There are several reasons radials are better. Because of the way they are constructed, nearly all radials are guaranteed for 40,000 miles. Under normal conditions, you should have no difficulty getting at least 60,000 miles from a set of good radials. This is at least three times the life of typical "bias-ply" tires. Radial tires also run considerably cooler than other tires, resulting in fewer blowouts and tire failures. My own experience indicates an added bonus: 6 percent to 8 percent better gas mileage.

If you are planning to keep your car for a while but need new tires, radials are the way to go. If possible, replace all four tires at the same time. I don't recommend using a bias-ply tire and a radial tire on the same axle, so you'll have to replace at least two tires when you switch. If you do replace only two of your four tires with radials, put them on the front wheels.

Many owner's manuals advise rotating your tires every few thousand miles to optimize wear. I don't recommend this. It simply isn't worth the time and money. If your car is properly aligned, you should have reasonably even tire wear.

The Right Pressure

Surveys have shown that one car in four has at least one seriously underinflated tire. A tire low on air will cause difficult steering, poor handling, reduced cargo capacity, and increased fuel consumption. It also will wear out sooner than a properly inflated tire.

You should check the pressure in your tires once a month with an accurate hand-held tire gauge. The gauges on the tire-inflation machines at gas stations aren't always accurate, so I suggest you buy one and keep it in the glove compartment.

Check the tires in the morning, before the car has

Checking Tire Pressure

Hold the tire gauge tightly against the valve.

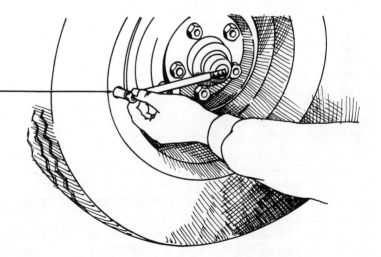

Are Tires a Good Buy?

A set of four premium radials can cost almost $500, including tax, mounting, and wheel balancing. That may sound like a lot of money, but it isn't when you compare it to other modes of transportation.

According to *Runner's World* magazine, driving is a better bargain than walking, at least as far as the cost of pounding pavement. A $500 set of radials, which lasts for at least 40,000 miles, costs you one and a quarter cents per mile. In comparison, a pair of average $35 jogging shoes, which should last for about 1,000 miles, cost you three and a half cents per mile—or nearly three times the cost of the tires.

been driven. After you've driven awhile, the tire heats up and the air expands, so you don't get an accurate reading. The manufacturer's recommended tire pressures are listed inside the glove compartment or on the driver's door. You may want to increase this pressure, however, as long as you don't exceed the maximum tire pressure written on the tire's sidewall. An increase of six pounds or so will increase your gas mileage. You may find the car runs a bit bumpier with the extra air, but in a short time you won't notice the difference.

Checking the tire pressure and adding air are done in the same way. Unscrew the cap from the tire valve. Hold the air-pump nozzle or the tire gauge against the valve tightly, so that no air hisses out. Then read the gauge and add air if necessary. Don't forget to replace the valve cap when you are finished—it keeps dirt out of the valve.

Remember: The air pressure in your tires will vary somewhat according to whether you've been driving and the outside air temperature. So check the pressure regularly to insure maximum performance.

Taking Care of Your Tires

In addition to checking the air pressure, you should inspect your tires at regular intervals for uneven wear,

Tire Problems

Underinflation
(worn tread on both edges)

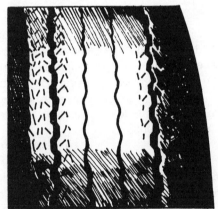

Overinflation
(worn tread in center)

Poor Alignment
(worn tread on one side)

especially in the front. (See the illustrations on page 61 for signs of improper tire wear.) Any signs of excessive tire wear on only one side of the car indicate an alignment problem. You should have the front-end alignment checked.

Here are the basic adjustments to tires and wheels:

■ **Wheel alignment**. This adjustment to the front wheels eliminates a shimmy in the steering wheel or pulling to one side when the car is on a straightaway.

■ **Wheel balancing** involves adding small weights to specific points on the wheel to eliminate vibrations, uneven treadwear, or poor handling.

■ **Caster adjustments.** These adjustments help the front wheels swing back to the straight-ahead position after you turn a corner. Too much caster makes it difficult to turn; too little can make it necessary for the driver to help the steering wheel return to its straight-ahead position.

■ **Toe-in adjustment.** This adjustment helps hold the car in a straight line. Too much toe-in can scuff your tires badly and make your car wander on the road. Excessive toe-out cannot be adjusted; it requires new parts.

■ **Camber adjustment.** This is a measurement of how far the front wheels tip in or out at the top. The adjustment varies, depending on what the manufacturer has found best for maximum tire life. It's not visible to the eye, and, like other wheel adjustments, requires a professional's precision equipment.

As I said earlier, your car's tires are your only contact with the ground. Never drive on worn-out tires. Even if they don't blow out, the slightest rain shower could cause a disaster, because your tires won't be able to grip the wet road adequately. Taking a few minutes to check the wear patterns and keep your tires properly inflated can add considerably to your driving pleasure—and put money in your pocket.

Chapter Two

Keeping Your Car in Shape

Keeping Your Car in Shape

A few hours of preventive maintenance can save you hundreds—or even thousands—of dollars a year. Regular care of both the minor mechanical items and the general appearance of your car will make it run better and last longer. Preventive maintenance not only will make driving more pleasurable, but will reduce the chances of an accident or major breakdown.

Keeping Good Records

Keeping accurate records of your car's maintenance and repair history isn't difficult if done on a regular basis, and it will make it easier to determine when the various systems of your car need attention. That can mean many extra dollars when you sell or trade in your car.

All you need is a small book to keep a diary of your car's repair history. You can buy one at most auto parts stores, or you can make your own, following the example on page 141. You also need a large envelope or file folder in which to keep repair and maintenance work orders, along with copies of warranties for tires, batteries, and other auto parts.

Recording repair costs and keeping receipts will pay dividends in many ways. If your car is used for business purposes, the records and receipts can be used for substantiating tax deductions. Besides knowing precisely when regular maintenance should be performed, good records can alert you to watch for special sales on items coming up for replacement, such as tires, oil, or shock absorbers. And properly kept records give you a true picture of what it actually costs to own and operate a car. Such information is essential to proper household budgeting.

Owner's manuals contain lists of suggested maintenance routines and their recommended frequencies. This is an excellent way to start developing your car's fitness program, although you may need to increase the frequency of some tasks depending on your driving habits and locale. If you live in a particularly hot and dusty climate, for example, you may need to increase the frequency of oil changes. The recommended frequency of most maintenance items is usually given in miles and time—6,000 miles or six months, for example. It is best to perform the indicated maintenance at the earlier of the two.

Once you establish a routine, it isn't difficult to take care of your car properly. If you haven't kept any records and aren't sure when something was last serviced, now is the time to start fresh. Invest the time and money it takes to get your car in tiptop shape and plan to keep it that way by performing maintenance at scheduled intervals. It's never too late to begin good car-maintenance habits.

Getting Started

Once you've decided to start a regular maintenance program, the first thing to do is a thorough visual inspection of your car. Go over the interior, the exterior, and the engine, making notes of any items needing

It's been said that the most neglected part of the car is the owner's manual. Many problems result from car owners not following the manufacturer's maintenance schedule, which is fully described in the manual.

special attention. Simple tasks can be performed at this time—such as checking and tightening all nuts, bolts, and screws.

For the most part, you won't need any special tools to accomplish this. Several "Phillips-head" screwdrivers and a set of open-end wrenches from $3/8$-inch to ¾-inch sizes usually will do the trick. (If you have a foreign car, you may need metric wrenches ranging from 10mm to 17mm.) This wil cover most fasteners you'll encounter. Tool kits available at many hardware and auto-parts stores include these basic tools in a handy carrying case. I strongly recommend you buy one.

Maintenance

Basic Starter Tools

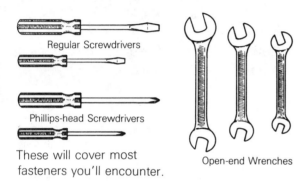

Regular Screwdrivers

Phillips-head Screwdrivers

These will cover most
fasteners you'll encounter.

Open-end Wrenches

It is surprising how many rattles and creaks disap-
pear after going over your car thoroughly. A little oil
or other lubricant applied to moving parts—hood,
trunk, and door hinges, for example—can work
wonders. Several easy-to-use aerosol products, including "silicone sprays," are widely available. One
such useful product, WD-40, has many applications.
   Some of the things worth checking:
■ Interior door panels and the dashboard. They

often are the sources of rattles that can drive you
crazy. The problem may be simply a loose screw.

■ Under the hood, check the battery, air cleaner,
and hoses. Other things—such as the distributor cap
or carburetor—may be loose, too, but you must be
careful—some screws in the engine are adjusting
screws; if you turn the wrong one, you could put
something out of adjustment.

   If your car is more than a year old, it is a good idea
to have your engine compartment cleaned. After
removing dirt and grime, it is much easier to locate
and identify oil and other fluid leaks in the various
engine systems. Many service stations will clean an
engine for less than $10, or you can do it yourself at
a car wash with a couple of cans of aerosol engine
cleaner and some hot water under pressure. (**Warning:** A process called "steam cleaning" gets the dirt
out of the engine compartment. It does an excellent
job of cleaning, but it sometimes can bring problems
to the surface. Loose or deteriorating hoses may
break or become unattached; poor electrical connec-

tions may ''short out''; some sealed areas may begin to leak.)

Looking Good, Inside and Out

In racing, we always say,''The best-looking cars are the best-running cars.''

I can't overemphasize the importance of keeping your car's interior and exterior looking clean and sharp. Not only will you enjoy driving more, but your efforts will pay enormous dividends when you sell or trade in your car.

Interior. The seats and carpet require frequent attention. Items such as the dashboard, door panels, and ceiling usually stay cleaner and require less maintenance.

Seats are easily kept clean by regular vacuuming and applying the proper cleaning product for the material. Fabric can be cleaned with any good upholstery cleaner. If your car is new, ''Scotchguarding'' the fabric can make it more stain-resistant and much easier to clean in the future.

I don't recommend covers to protect the seats.

They detract from the beauty and enjoyment of the car. Moreover, some fabrics are adversely affected by vinyl covers, which trap moisture and don't allow the upholstery to breathe.

Vinyl probably is the most practical seat material to maintain. It is easy to clean with any number of good spray products available in auto, drug, and grocery stores. After cleaning, an application of vinyl protective spray will keep it soft and looking new.

For leather, saddle soap works best. It keeps leather pliable and helps inhibit the natural cracks that appear when leather starts to dry out.

Be careful: Many vinyl and leather protective sprays contain silicone and other ingredients harmful to window tint film. When applying these products, avoid getting them on your film-tinted windows. In such cases, it's wiser to spray the solution on a clean rag and then apply it to the upholstery.

Carpets require regular and frequent vacuuming. Small, battery-operated vacuums simply won't do the job. A good home vacuum with the proper attachment probably will suffice. The more powerful coin-operated machines at car washes and service stations are better.

Carpet stains should be removed as soon as possible using any of the many products available. Your favorite rug shampoo will work just fine for general cleaning. If you have floor mats, they should be removed regularly and the underlying carpet vacuumed thoroughly.

Door panels are made of a variety of materials. Vinyl and fabric can be treated much the same as seat material. Some door panels have plastic sections that may be cleaned with mild detergent and water; your vinyl cleaner generally will do the job if dirt is not imbedded in the material. After cleaning the plastic, a

Touch-Ups

Even the most careful drivers get their share of parking-lot scratches and paint chipping. The sooner you tend to these minor abrasions, the easier it will be to cover them up. A chip that is left too long can turn into a rust spot—and a more difficult repair.

Most auto-parts stores and dealers carry touch-up paint for the color of your car. Be sure to match the manufacturer's brand. Depending on the car's age and condition, the touch-up paint may not exactly match the rest of your car. If your car usually is parked outside, sunlight and other elements may have caused the original paint to fade; when you add the touch-up paint, it may stand out. That's another reason touch-ups should be applied as quickly as possible.

The area to be touched up should be cleaned well. Use a wax and grease remover on the area. If it's not clean, the new paint won't adhere properly. After the touch-up paint has dried, use a rubbing compound to blend the new paint into the rest of the car. Cover the repaired area with a good coat of wax; this new paint isn't as thick as the rest of the finish and will be more vulnerable to the elements.

treatment with your vinyl protective spray is in order.

Headliners—the interior ceiling—seldom accumulate dirt and need very little attention. If yours is vinyl, an occasional cleaning and coating with your vinyl protective product is all that is needed.

Dashboards should be cleaned regularly with your vinyl cleaner or a mixture of mild detergent and water. A liberal coating of vinyl protective spray on a frequent basis helps prevent cracking caused by sunlight. This same treatment usually will keep any chrome or brass trim on the dash looking good. If ashtrays are used, they should be cleaned regularly to minimize odors. If the gauges on the dashboard are covered with glass, use a glass cleaner; if plastic, use an all-purpose cleaner.

Exterior. The most obvious sign of a well-maintained car is a bright and shiny exterior. A sharp exterior is very important when you decide to sell your car because it is the first thing the potential buyer sees. No exterior will last forever, of course, but here are some measures that will substantially lengthen the lifespan of your car's finish.

Washing your car regularly is a good place to start. But exactly *how* you wash depends partly on the quality of your local water. If you have "hard" water, rings and film may be left on your car's surface. Because it is difficult to change the water supply, the next best thing is to dry the car before the water can evaporate.

Don't use detergent or common coarse soaps. Harsh detergents cause your car's paint to lose its residual oils. Use a nondetergent soap made especially for waxed surfaces or a liquid soap used for dishwashing by hand.

Use a nozzle with as much pressure as possible to dislodge dirt. Be sure to rinse the car thoroughly. Start washing your car from the top and work down. Abrasive dirt tends to flow down and away from parts you have already washed, resulting in less scratching of the surface. The best washing tool is a sponge, some type of car-wash mitten, or a soft towel. Whichever you use, keep it clean by rinsing frequently or replace it whenever it becomes dirty.

Try not to wash your car in direct sunlight, when the surface is extremely hot. Remove tree sap or bird droppings immediately, because they have a tendency to eat through the paint.

The wheels and tires should be washed last. Use a bristle brush designed for this purpose, or a household brush that isn't too abrasive. Spray water up inside the wheel wells and under the rocker panels. Salt and debris can get trapped there and cause rust.

When drying the car, use fluffy terry towels. A chamois will work well, but it also can drag dirt particles along with the water. Start drying at the top and work your way down.

Waxing is the next step, but you need to be careful about which of the many different products you choose.

Cleaners are made to remove the dirt from the top surface of the paint. Cleaners have no protective qualities; they clean the surface but don't protect it. **Rubbing compounds** or **polishing compounds** are used to remove stubborn stains and dirt as well as minor imperfections, scratches, and badly weathered paint. **Polishes** usually do not contain abrasives or waxes; they merely shine the paint by adding oils to it. **Waxes** are used as a protective coating for the paint and polish. The use of liquid, paste, or hard wax is a personal choice, but if protection is all you seek, use whichever is easiest to apply.

Oxidation—exposure to air—is paint's biggest enemy. You can't stop oxidation completely, but conscientious use of polishes and waxes definitely will slow it down. Follow directions carefully and don't assume that if a little is good, a lot is better. When you apply a second or third layer of wax, you remove the wax you just applied. Remember that all products aren't suitable for all finishes. Read the label before buying. Many products come with their own applicators. You also may buy separate applicator pads at auto-supply sections of grocery and department stores. A clean piece of Turkish toweling or terry cloth will work well.

> *Keep a notebook with a pen or pencil in your glove compartment. It will come in handy from time to time.*

Here are some more tips on waxing your car:

■ For best results, work in the shade or your garage.

■ Clean or turn the applicator often to avoid contaminating one part of the car with debris from a previously waxed section.

■ Always apply the wax to the pad, not to the car.

■ Apply sparingly. Follow the directions as to the proper motion—circular or back-and-forth. If the directions don't specify, use a back-and-forth motion; a circular motion can leave swirl marks.

■ Allow the wax to dry thoroughly before buffing. If you buff too soon, your car will end up with a dull finish.

■ Use plenty of clean towels to remove the dried wax. Shake out and turn the towels often.

How often you wax your car depends on climate

Exterior Checklist

■ Look for chips, scratches, and dents. If you find visible damage, decide whether you can do the repair work yourself or need professional help.
■ Make sure all trim is sealed evenly. If not, use "silicone sealer" or another appropriate adhesive to reseal all loose areas. Moisture can get trapped in these areas and cause rust.
■ Check all rubber and vinyl trim—such as bumpers, door guards, and weather-stripping—for signs of deterioration. A quick cleaning and application of a vinyl protectant is recommended.
■ Look for chrome, vinyl, or weather-stripping that needs replacement. Check also the condition of the windshield-wiper blades. These items are available at auto-parts stores and new-car dealers.

Maintenance

and driving conditions. The harsher the conditions and climate, the more often you should wax. In most areas, twice-a-year waxing is sufficient.

How do you know your car needs waxing? Simple:

If water beads readily on your car's surface, the wax is still doing its job. If not, you're overdue for another coat.

Here are some areas to which you should pay special attention:

Chrome. These days, everything with a mirror finish on your car isn't necessarily chrome. Much aluminum, plastic, and stainless-steel trim is used, and not all chrome cleaners are good for these materials. Check the product's label to see on what surfaces it should—and shouldn't—be used. A good wax, however, can be used on most painted and metal parts.

Windows. Any good glass cleaner will suffice. A product called "Rain-X" puts a protective coating on the outside of your windshield that allows water to drain off more quickly. It improves visibility in the rain, especially if your windshield wipers aren't in perfect condition. I use this product when racing, and it works very well. White vinegar and water works, too.

Vinyl roofs. Vinyl roofs can do wonders for a car's appearance—as long as they are cared for regularly. A vinyl top must be washed frequently, thoroughly, and vigorously. Use a mild detergent and a brush. Liberal applications of a good vinyl protective spray help ward off the ravages of sun, heat, dirt, and pollution. Any rips, tears, or loose edges should be repaired at once. Moisture that gets between the vinyl and the metal underneath can cause rust. You'll see evidence in the form of tiny bubbles popping up under the vinyl. At this point, your only remedy generally is to replace the top.

Rubber trim. Increasing amounts of rubber are being used on car exteriors. Wax on these areas is not recommended. A number of good vinyl cleaners also work well on rubber. It is important not only to clean rubber, but to keep it protected from cracking and chipping.

Chapter Three

Dealing with a Mechanic

Dealing with a Mechanic

Americans spend more than $40 billion a year to repair and maintain their cars. That's a lot. Also large is the number of customer complaints about mechanics to federal, state, and local consumer-affairs offices, Better Business Bureaus, and other consumer-protection organizations.

That need not be. There are several things you can do to maximize your chances for satisfaction and minimize your chances of being victimized by an unscrupulous repair shop.

Most auto mechanics are skilled, honest, hard-working people like you and me. And they want to give you exactly what you want: good service at a fair price. So where can you find such service? The answer begins with an understanding of the different types of service facilities. Each has its own benefits and drawbacks. Let's take a brief tour:

Dealerships are good if your car is still under warranty or if it needs an extensive repair requiring original parts from the manufacturer. Such repairs might involve the engine, transmission, or steering. Because dealers have close associations with car manufacturers, they generally have the proper tools, parts inventory, factory training, and the latest service information for your particular model car. On they other hand, they often are more expensive than independent shops because they have larger facilities and bigger overhead. Moreover, some dealers are more concerned with selling cars than fixing them, so you may not get as much personal attention as you would from a shop where repairs are its only business.

Chain stores such as Sears, Montgomery Ward, and K-Mart often advertise specials on certain repairs, offering bargains for smart shoppers. Many are open longer hours, including weekends, than dealers or other repair shops. And they generally provide an acceptable warranty for parts and labor (more on that later). But be careful: Those "bargains" sometimes are narrowly defined. For example, a $19.95 tune-up may apply only to four-cylinder American-made cars. If you've got a bigger car or an import, you'll have to pay extra. Some "specials" don't include parts; others don't include labor. You have to ask. Another disadvantage of chain-store shops is that their personnel are not always as well trained as they should be, and there generally is a high turnover of employees. Some chain stores are limited to certain types of repairs, or to certain car models. But for regular maintenance and repairs—such as tune-ups, brake jobs, muffler replacement, or front-end alignment—these shops may offer good service at a good price.

Independent repair shops often are more concerned with their reputations because their business depends largely on word of mouth. Many are privately owned (frequently, one of the mechanics is the owner) so you may have more one-on-one contact with mechanics and their boss. Many such shops specialize in a particular make and model of automobile and have in-depth knowledge of that car's

When it comes to automobile repair and maintenance, there is no correlation between price and quality of workmanship. This has been documented in study after study.

problems and solutions to these problems, as well as a good inventory of parts. Independent shops, however, are not always up to date on the latest technical information, techniques, and equipment.

With independents, it's even more important to get estimates in writing, along with any warranties for parts or labor. It doesn't hurt to check in advance with a local Better Business Bureau and with a local city or county office of consumer affairs. Independents also tend to run behind schedule on completion of the work promised. The best recommendations, of course, are from friends who are satisfied customers.

Service stations are usually the most convenient source for repairs. They often are less expensive than other shops for routine jobs and can be an excellent

Mechanics

source of information when you need to diagnose a problem. Few shops, however, are adequately equipped to handle complicated jobs. And service station personnel have a tendency to commit to more than they can deliver. Be sure to find out what warranties they offer. *Note:* Several oil companies have consumer-protection clauses in their leases with service-station franchisees. If several complaints are registered against a service station, its license with the oil company could be terminated. Some oil-company-affiliated stations offer competitive prices and good warranties. As always, it helps to get all promises in writing. With the increase of self-service gas stations, fewer service stations actually offer repair services these days.

Specialty shops usually limit their service to one or two areas, such as mufflers, tires, or brakes. They frequently feature specials, are open long hours, and have many locations in some metropolitan areas. In addition, they usually work quickly and their guarantees often are excellent. But these shops may try to sell you more than you need. And the quality of mechanics can be spotty from shop to shop.

The Right Shop with the Right Stuff

Here are some tips for finding the right shop:

■ Ask co-workers, neighbors, friends, and friends of friends for recommendations. When you call the shop, make it clear you are coming to them on the recommendation of another customer. That way, the shop will know it has to please *two* customers.

■ Call several shops to get an estimate. Besides finding out who charges what, you may learn other things about the shop, particularly how courteous shop personnel are to potential new customers. It may be a good indication of how they'll treat you later on. Don't necessarily go for the lowest price. A good rule of thumb is to eliminate the highest and lowest estimates. The former is probably charging too much; the latter may be cutting too many corners.

■ Check with the Better Business Bureau and a local consumer affairs office. But don't take their word as gospel—there are many shops both good and bad about which they've never heard. But if their report

> *If you get to know a mechanic employed by a repair shop, don't be afraid to ask if he or she is available for work on the side, such as evenings or weekends. The labor will be cheaper.*

about a shop isn't favorable, you can safely omit it from your list.

■ Inspect the shop for neatness and cleanliness. Keep in mind that car-repair work is dirty, but a well-kept shop indicates pride in workmanship.

■ Talk to the mechanic or the service manager. A good shop's employees will have an interest in your car, take the time to find out exactly what's wrong, and explain things to you clearly. If you're not satisfied with the attention you get, go elsewhere.

■ Check for licensing (with a city, county, or state agency) and certification (with the National Institute for Automotive Service Excellence, the American Automobile Association, or another organization).

How to Talk to a Mechanic

Men frequently are uncomfortable when setting foot in traditionally feminine territory—like the lingerie section of a department store—so there is nothing unusual about women not feeling comfortable in a auto repair shop, service station, or dealer service department. With a little bit of knowledge and self-confidence, women can deal with mechanics just as well as with anyone else.

Here's what to do:

■ Be informed. The more information you can provide about what is wrong with your car, the more confidently you will communicate your problem, and the better your chances for successful repairs.

■ Provide documentation about the problem. If possible, keep an informal diary of you car's symptoms: the type of problem, whether it occurs when the engine is cold or warm, at high speeds or low

Mechanics

What Is a Tune-Up?

Time for a tune-up? Before you take your car to a mechanic and ask for one, you'd better determine exactly what a tune-up is.

Every mechanic seems to have a different definition of "tune-up." There are "minor tune-ups" and "major tune-ups," but even these differ from mechanic to mechanic.

The most common tune-up includes:

■ replacing the sparkplugs;
■ replacing the points;
■ replacing the air filter;
■ replacing the fuel filter; and
■ adjusting the carburetor.

That's a start, but it isn't enough to guarantee your car a long and happy life. Here's what I think a complete tune-up should include:

■ replacing the sparkplugs;
■ replacing the points;
■ replacing the air filter;
■ replacing the fuel filter;
■ adjusting the carburetor;
■ checking all belts, hoses, and wires;
■ checking all fluid levels and adding or changing where necessary;
■ cleaning and servicing pollution-control devices; and
■ testing the distributor or the electrical ignition system.

The difference between these two tune-ups is mostly labor and attention to detail. The extra checking will cost a little extra, but you should save money by improving fuel economy and the life of your car. And, as you can see, you can do many of these things yourself.

speeds, when turning, stopping, accelerating, or at any other time. Careful notes can provide a mechanic with valuable information that can save you a great deal in repair costs. See the trouble-shooting guide on page 132 for help in diagnosing the probable causes of several common car problems.

■ Try to talk to the person who actually will be doing the work. Be very specific when describing your car's problems and ask a lot of specific questions about the repair work to be done.

■ Try to sound knowledgeable, but don't overdo it. Don't show off by trying to sound smarter than you are. You'll only get into trouble.

■ Get a written estimate. If the mechanic insists on looking at the car before giving you an estimate, that's okay—no mechanic can tell you everything that's wrong from your description or simply by looking under the hood. But make it clear you won't pay for any work done until you have an estimate. Many shops charge a nominal fee if their mechanics must

It's a good idea to make an appointment for any car repair, just as you do for the dentist, hairdresser, veterinarian, or other professional. Auto-shop owners appreciate your consideration in calling in advance and usually give you priority service.

take your car apart to determine the problem and you later decide not to have them do the work. Whatever you do, don't sign a ''blank check'' by authorizing the shop to do whatever is necessary to fix your car.

■ Get a second (or even a third) opinion for repairs likely to cost more than $100. During this search, you may even find a shop you feel more confident working with.

When You Pick Up Your Car

It's best to call ahead to make sure your car is ready. This is simple courtesy, and it could save you an unnecessary trip.

Mechanics

Questions to Ask Your Mechanic

"How critical is this repair?" Sometimes, a repair suggested by a mechanic isn't urgent. If you know you will be selling or trading in your car within a year, you may want to forgo some less urgent repairs.

"What alternatives are available to 'replacing it with a new one?'" There often are several, such as replacing it with a "rebuilt" or "reworked" part, or one taken from a junked car. The old item itself sometimes can be repaired.

"What effect will the repair have on other components in the system?" It won't help to get new tires if your shock absorbers are bad, causing excessive tire wear. Repairs often can affect related components.

"Can the work be spread out?" If major work is required, it sometimes can be spread out over several months, with small portions being done at each of several visits. This may help you better budget your money and avoid giving up your car for an extended period.

"Is it possible to adjust something before replacing it?" Some mechanics have a tendency to "rip and replace" when a rather minor adjustment may be all that's necessary. This may be especially applicable to the carburetor and other parts of the fuel system.

"What would you do if it was your car?" When there are several options, this simple question to the mechanic may bring a surprising response. It may turn out that the mechanic would go for the simplest, least expensive repair. It's worth asking.

> *If you're happy with a mechanic's work, compliment the mechanic and ask for him (or her) the next time you come in. You'll get to know each other, and the mechanic will get to know your car.*

When you get your bill, inspect the work order. Make sure the work done was specified on the written estimate and the price is close to what you were quoted. Most state laws specify that if the repair bill exceeds the original estimate by a certain amount—say, $25 or 5 percent of the estimate—you are not liable for those additional charges.

If you had a specific problem, take a test drive to make certain it's been solved. With some repairs, you will be able to tell immediately whether a problem has been taken care of. If you take a spin around the block and the problem is still there, you should not have to pay for the work—at least not until it is done to your satisfaction. If the problem returns a few days after the repair was done, bring the car back to the shop immediately.

You may want to ask for the old parts. If you're at all suspicious whether old parts actually were replaced, put a piece of tape or otherwise mark any parts you know will be replaced. Then look for the mark on the used parts when you pick up your car.

The final bill should include:

■ your name and address;
■ the name and address of the shop;
■ the date of the repairs;
■ your car make, model, registration, and mileage;
■ an itemized list of repairs;
■ descriptions of parts used in the repairs, including whether the parts are new or rebuilt;
■ total parts charges;
■ total labor charges, including how many hours at what hourly rate;
■ total charges; and
■ warranties for parts and labor for all work done.

Don't be afraid to point out problems. If anything doesn't meet with your approval, speak to someone with authority. Be polite but firm and remain calm.

Paying by credit card may help you if a problem turns up later on. If there is a dispute about the quali-

Mechanics

ty of repairs, federal law allows you to withhold payment, giving you leverage with the shop to remedy problems. But you may withhold only the portion of the bill under dispute and must carefully follow certain other procedures, described periodically in your credit-card bill. If you can't pay by credit card, make a notation on the bill (your copy and the shop's) that there is a dispute. If you don't pay the bill in full, the shop may not be required to release your car to you.

If You're Not Satisfied

You have certain rights under state and federal law to protect yourself against shoddy workmanship or unauthorized repairs. But you must do certain things to protect yourself. Here are some tips:

■ Talk to the manager, owner, or some other person in charge. It is important that you make every reasonable effort to solve the problem directly with the shop. Write down the name of anyone you talk to, along with a brief summary of your conversation. This may come in handy later on.

Four Golden Rules

1. Acquire some basic knowledge about how your car works. There is no substitute for an informed consumer.
2. Describe your car's problems accurately and in detail (when the problem occurs, how often, the kind of noise it makes, and so on).
3. Use your best judgment and follow your common sense.
4. Establish a good relationship with your mechanic or service manager. Confidence means trusting not just yourself, but someone who can help you.

■ Write a letter to the shop, describing the situation in detail. Make it clear you intend to get action. But don't be threatening. You may want to send copies of the letter to a local Better Business Bureau, a government consumer agency, private consumer groups, and the state attorney general's office. If you do send copies, note this fact at the bottom of your letter. Always keep a copy for yourself, of course.

■ If the shop is affiliated with an automobile manufacturer or a national chain, send a copy to the regional or national manager. Ford, General Motors, Chrysler, and most other auto makers have complaint-resolution programs.

■ Consider small-claims court. If you don't receive satisfaction, this may be a low-cost way to obtain justice. Filing suit in small-claims court generally costs under $30. The proceedings are relatively informal and you don't need an attorney, although it's possible the shop will send one anyway. Best of all, small-claims courts usually render quick decisions and often favor consumers.

Mechanics

Chapter Four

How to Buy a Car

How to Buy a Car

Everyone has a horror story about a visit to a car dealer. The stories have a similar theme: No one will talk to you and those who will insult you by treating you like a helpless child.

There is no excuse or justification for improper treatment by car salespeople. If it does occur, I urge you to bring it politely to the attention of the manager, making it clear you won't stand for such behavior.

The most important thing to remember is: *You should buy a car—not be sold a car.*

If you go out to *buy* a $600 refrigerator and a salesperson *sells* you a top-of-the-line model for $800, you may not be happy about spending the extra money. You may even resent your purchase every time you use it. But, if after careful consideration, *you decided* you wanted the more expensive model, you'd probably be thankful the salesperson took the time to show you the extra features.

Be sure you are buying what you want and need—not what the salesperson wants to sell you. But also be sure to take advantage of a salesperson's expertise by getting enough specific information to make the right choice.

Your choice of a car should reflect your current and future needs. Your first task, then, is to sit down in a comfortable environment and do a little homework. Make two lists. On one, describe your needs. On the other, list the features and options you want and need in a car, preferably in order of priority.

Here are some questions to ask yourself when making up the first of the two lists:

■ How will the car be used? For what will it be used most?

Work:_____ miles per month
Shopping:_____ miles per month
Children:_____ miles per month
Pleasure:_____ miles per month

Annual Gas Costs

(based on driving 10,000 miles a year)

price per gallon

mpg	$1.20	$1.30	$1.40	$1.50
15	$800	$867	$933	$1000
20	600	650	700	750
25	480	520	560	600
30	400	433	467	500
35	343	371	400	429
40	300	325	350	375
45	267	289	311	333
50	240	260	280	300

■ How many people does the car need to hold comfortably? (Will this number change in the next three to five years?)

■ What are my priorities in a car? (Rank in order of preference.)
Performance_____
Comfort_____
Economy_____
Safety_____
Luxury_____

■ How much can I spend each month on gas? (See chart at left.)

■ Who will be driving the car? (Consider size differences, the adjustability of the driver's seat and steering, and manual vs. automatic transmission.)

■ Will anything in the next few years affect my automotive needs? (A marriage or children could shift needs from a small car to a larger one. A change in jobs or assignments could increase commuting.)

Buying a Car

Look around at other cars on the street. Which do you like? Even more important, which *don't* you like? Ask friends, relatives, neighbors, and others what cars they drive, what they like and don't like about their cars, and where they bought them.

One more tip. If you need to rent a car, request a model you are considering buying. It's a good way to get some basic information, along with an extended test drive. Keep in mind that rental companies generally buy stripped-down models with few amenities and that these cars probably have been abused by previous renters.

Big Car or Small?

Here are some pros and cons of the five principal classes of cars. Of course, what's really ''pro'' or ''con'' depends a lot on your own tastes and needs.

Subcompact
(Base price: $4,000 - $8,000)

Pro
Lowest cost
Seats two; maybe four
Easy to handle, park
Fuel-efficient
Low operating,
  maintenance costs

Con
Rougher ride
Limited cargo space
Lacks acceleration
Not comfortable for long
  trips

> *Record the serial number of your car keys so you can get them replaced easily and quickly. The number is stamped directly on the master key that comes with the car.*

Compact
(Base price: $4,500 - $9,000)

Pro
Low initial cost
Seats four comfortably
Easy to handle, park
Low operating, main-
  tenance costs
Excellent for commuting

Con
Not as comfortable ride
  as larger cars
Limited cargo space
Limited availability of
  high-comfort features

Intermediate
(Base price: $5,000 - $9,000)

Pro
Good value
Good room and comfort
Moderate operating,
  maintenance costs
Seats six fairly com-
  fortably
Good choice of engines,
  options
Good road stability on
  highways

Con
Not spacious for big
  families
Somewhat harder to han-
  dle and park
Not all that fuel-efficient

Buying a Car

Full-Size
(Base price: $5,500 - $9,000)

Pro
Good stability and
  comfort
Seats six comfortably
Good for long trips
Able to tow heavy loads
Lots of cargo space
Wide choice of options

Con
Relatively expensive to
  buy, operate, maintain
Low fuel economy
Hard to handle and park
May come with more options
  than you want or need

Luxury
(Base price: $10,000 and up)

Pro
Excellent comfort
Seats four to six com-
  fortably
Excellent for long trips
Every feature available

Con
Expensive
Low fuel economy
Less cargo and passenger
  space than full-size cars
Hard to handle and park

Establishing a Budget

This isn't as simple as it seems. To understand how much your car will really cost each month, it's important to know not just the amount of your loan payment, but all the other costs associated with owning, operating, and maintaining an automobile. Here's a rundown of some of the costs:

Loan payments. This clearly is your biggest cost. The exact amount depends on several things, including the size of the loan, the interest rate, and the number of years the loan will last. On the next page are monthly payments for loans at several interest rates for three and four years. To find out the exact amount of a loan for a car you are considering—based on current interest rates and other terms—call a local bank.

Insurance. You can get insurance rates easily by calling a local agent. Rates depend partly on the type of car you buy. Sports cars, for example, have higher accident rates, so insurance premiums usually are higher. Cars with stronger bumpers and other safety features may qualify for lower premiums. Other determining factors include engine size, the number of doors, the type of roof, and whether you will use the car for commuting to work. Of course, other things, including your age and driving record, also affect insurance rates.

Other considerations when buying insurance:

■ How much deductible for collision coverage do you need? (If you can raise your deductible from, say, $100 to $300, you could cut your insurance costs substantially.)
■ Does your state require a minimum amount of liability coverage?
■ Do you qualify for discounts offered by many insurance companies to nonsmokers, students, senior citizens, and those in other special categories?

Finally, automobile coverage varies widely from company to company. It is important to comparison-shop among at least three different insurance companies.

Maintenance and repairs. This is a major cost in car ownership. A good rule of thumb is to budget $50 per month for maintenance and repairs. You won't spend anything in some months, but you'll

Monthly Loan Payments

Amount of Loan	Interest Rate	Monthly Payment 3-year loan	4-year loan
$ 6,000	10%	$193.61	$152.18
8,000		258.14	202.91
10,000		322.68	253.63
12,000		387.21	304.96
$ 6,000	12%	$199.29	$158.01
8,000		265.72	210.68
10,000		332.15	263.34
12,000		398.58	316.01
$ 6,000	14%	$205.07	$ 163.96
8,000		273.43	218.62
10,000		341.78	273.27
12,000		410.14	327.92
$ 6,000	16%	$210.95	$170.05
8,000		281.26	226.73
10,000		351.58	283.41
12,000		421.89	340.09

Buying a Car

make up for it later, when it's time for a major repair.

Other costs. These include parking, tolls, taxes, license, and inspection fees.

The bottom line. According to a survey by the federal government, it costs about 19 cents per mile to own and operate a subcompact, about 21 cents per mile for a compact car, about 24 cents per mile for an intermediate-sized car, and about 27 cents per mile for a large car. These costs include depreciation, maintenance, gas, oil, parking, tolls, insurance, and taxes. If you drive 10,000 miles per year, those annual costs, using the government's averages, would range from $1,900 to $2,700 per year. The government's figures, however, do not include loan payments and interest.

Gathering Information

There's no question about it—there's a direct relationship between adequate information and a satisfactory decision. The more you can find out about which car will best suit your wants and needs, the more likely it is you'll find the "right" car.

When shopping for automobile insurance, make sure you receive any discounts for which you qualify. Discounts are available for nonsmokers, for students away at school, for drivers who participate in car pools, and for owners of cars with crash-resistant bumpers, among other categories. But you won't get any discounts if you don't ask.

The more you read, the better. Information about car makes and models is almost endless. Company brochures on new cars, for example, are available in dealer showrooms. Several magazines rate new and used cars, including *Consumer Reports, Autoweek, Road & Track, Car & Driver, Motor Trend, Road Test*, and *Popular Mechanics*. You can find most of these at a magazine store, or at a library, where you can scan back issues. You also can write to the magazines to request back issues.

After you've looked at a few cars and read some literature, you can begin to make a "shopping list" of options and features you need and want. You'll soon have a good checklist against which to judge any potential purchase. Do you want power steering? Rear window defroster? AM/FM/cassette stereo? Air conditioning? Try to rank these items in order of preference. If your "dream car" turns out to be more than you can afford, this can help you eliminate some items. Or if you find a car that has some but not all of these features, your list can remind you whether the car has the features you feel are most important.

Weighing the various options can be difficult. Here are some things to consider:

■ Automatic vs. manual transmission. Automatic transmissions eliminate manually shifting gears, but manual transmissions offer better acceleration, speed control, and fuel economy.

■ Radial tires. As I mentioned in Chapter Two, radials last longer, offer better fuel economy, and generally provide better handling. They also are more expensive.

■ Air conditioning. This gives obvious comfort in hot weather, but also drains power from the engine and reduces fuel economy by up to 10 percent.

■ Radios and tape players. The choices are almost endless. Your decision should depend on what you generally listen to and how important a "sound system" is to you. If you listen primarily to radio news and talk shows, a high-performance audiophile system will be a waste of money.

■ Power steering and brakes. This is a must for larger cars, but may not be necessary on smaller, lighter cars, which are easier to maneuver and stop. A test drive can help you decide.

■ Cruise control. This option allows you to maintain a desired speed on highways. It's great if you take a lot of long trips, but unnecessary for city driving.

■ Tilt steering wheel. This allows you to raise and lower the steering column to accommodate drivers of different sizes. If you're the only driver, you probably don't need it.

Buying a Car

Options Shopping List

Here are some of the more popular options and their approximate manufacturer's suggested retail prices:

Air conditioning	$560–710	Power steering	$170–195
Automatic speed control	140–155	Power windows	150–220
Automatic transmission	370–400	Radios:	
Clock	25–60	AM/FM radio	50–70
Dual remote-control mirrors	40–65	AM/FM stereo radio	85–110
Electric rear-window defroster	100–125	AM/FM stereo with cassette player	170–300
Electric trunk-lid release	20–45	AM/FM stereo with 8-track player	160–175
Extended service plan	175–670	Tilt steering wheel	85–105
Heavy-duty battery	20–30	Tilt-up moon roof	240–255
Illuminated entry system	60–75	Tinted glass	75–100
Interval windshield wipers	45–60	Two-tone paint	85–185
Power brakes	75–95	Vinyl roof	125–165
Power door locks	120–185	Wire wheel covers	125–155
Power seat	130–195		

■ Illuminated entry. This excellent safety feature lights up your car's interior when you put the key in the door.

One often overlooked option is an extended service plan. This protects you after your original new-vehicle service plan expires. Each manufacturer's plan is different, so be sure to check all the details. Depending on your personal driving habits and coverage needs, you may select from a three-year, 36,000-mile plan to a five-year, 50,000-mile plan. It is important to find out if the policy is transferable when you sell your car. If so, it will increase the car's resale value.

Getting the Best Price

Once you've decided which car you want and have established a budget, it's time to make your move.

If you are buying a new car, it's important to shop around among several dealerships. Unlike buying a coat, toaster, or almost anything else, the price of an automobile is negotiable—up to a point, that is. A dealer pays a wholesale price for a car and sells it to you for another price. The difference between the wholesale and retail prices is the negotiable margin. The margin can vary—from about $200 to more than $1,000—depending on the size of the car, its price range, and demand.

Remember that you're not shopping merely for the best price. You also must consider the dealer's service department and the convenience of the dealer to you, because you probably will have to bring the car back for periodic check-ups. It may be worth spending a few extra dollars for convenience and good service. (See "Dealing With Dealers," page 98.)

When you compare prices, be sure you are comparing apples with apples. That means comparing two cars with identical options.

Another key consideration is the trade-in allowance you get on your present car. There may be big differences among dealers, because one might be interested in reconditioning the car and reselling it at a higher price while another might want to sell it quickly "as is" at a low price. One dealer might offer a pittance for your trade-in, but give you an excellent price on your new car; another might do the op-

Buying a Car

posite. The ''bottom-line'' price is what you should compare.

I strongly urge you to consider selling your car yourself, through a newspaper ad or some other means, because you usually can get more for it than through a dealer trade-in. (More on selling a car in the next chapter.)

By the way, get price quotations in writing. Besides having a firm quote, the written material will be useful when comparison shopping.

When you order specific options for a new car, it sometimes means you can't get your car right away from the dealer's inventory; the car must be special-ordered from the manufacturer. If that's the case, fine, but consider choosing a car from the dealer's lot with *almost* everything you wanted. You may get a much better price because the dealer already has paid for the car and wants to get repaid as quickly as possible. You always can add certain options later.

Moreover, many dealers—of both new and used cars—subscribe to computerized networks that allow them to find other dealers that might have the car you are looking for. Ask if your dealer can do this.

A final word about price. Just as with seasonal sales at department stores, you are likely to get a better deal on cars at certain times of the year. The end of a model year—usually late summer—is one good time, because dealers are trying to clear their showrooms of ''last year's models.'' The end of the month also is good, because that is when salespeople have extra pressure to meet sales quotas.

Taking a Test Drive

There are two times it is essential you take a test drive: before you make a final purchase decision and again when you pick up your car.

Before you buy, test drive a car to analyze how well you fit in the seat and the visibility out the front, side, and rear windows. Some other things you'll want to consider:

- how smoothly the car rides;
- how well it responds to your steering efforts;
- how quickly it accelerates when passing;
- how quickly it stops;

■ how easy it is to park;
■ how well the heater and air conditioner work; and
■ the quietness of the ride.

Review the "shopping list" you made earlier to see how well this car measures up to your "dream car."

The test drive allows you to get to know a car before you decide to buy it. Be as thorough as possible. Don't merely drive it around the block. Try to duplicate your normal driving conditions: parking, city driving, highway driving, whatever.

If any questions arise during the test drive, bring them up immediately with the salesperson. After you arrive back at the dealership, sit in the car for a few minutes with the salesperson and go over your questions.

It is very important to test drive your new car at the time of delivery. Ask the salesperson to go with you and to explain how the car operates—how to use the heater, horn, and turn signals; how to open the hood; how to make the seats recline; and so on. You should know all of these things before leaving the dealership.

Equally important is to examine the car carefully for defects and for optional items you cannot locate. Take the time to discuss these with the salesperson. You've just spent a lot of money and you deserve some time, consideration, and courtesy.

Trading In

One important consideration is how much your present car may be worth. Depending on several factors, it can shave hundreds or even thousands of dollars from the price of your new car. You'll need to decide whether to trade in your old car to the dealer, or to sell it privately and apply the money to your new car. See Chapter Five for more on selling your car.

Let's recap the process. You have (1) analyzed your needs, (2) established a budget, (3) gathered brochures and other consumer information, (4) made a list of features and options in their order of importance, (5) shopped around for the best price, and (6) taken some test drives. Once you've decided which car you want, it's time to choose the dealer from which to buy it.

Buying a Car

Dealing with Dealers

Finding the right dealer is one of the most important steps in buying a car. A good dealer will be able to answer questions about your car — before and after you buy it. And, of course, a good dealer will provide unfailingly good service.

It's important that you trust your dealer. When you first set foot in the showroom, you can begin to evaluate the business.

- Are cars displayed attractively?
- Are personnel friendly and courteous?
- Is the place clean and neat?
- Is the dealership conveniently located? Does it have convenient business hours?
- Does the dealer provide ''loaner'' cars or special rental rates when yours is in the shop?
- Are your questions answered and phone calls returned promptly?

It may be helpful to ask local business contacts, friends, and neighbors about their experiences with the dealer, as well as for any background information they may have. An increasing number of dealers have gone out of business in recent years, so this background information may be important.

A dealer should be committed to providing excellent service. Don't settle for less.

Closing the Deal

When the time comes for the final purchase, you will be asked to fill out and sign several things. Let's review the final paperwork:

Buyer's order. This is a full written description of the car, including base price, option costs, dealer fees, and taxes. This is written up when you agree verbally to buy a specific vehicle. *It is not a legally binding document.* You usually will be asked to leave a deposit with the salesperson, which may be refundable if you decide not to complete the purchase. But you must make certain the deposit is refundable by having this written into the buyer's order. And don't sign the order until all of the terms are acceptable to you. Don't accept any promises that aren't in writing.

Title application. This legal document registers your

car with a state licensing agency. It includes the buyer's name and address, the vehicle identification number, a description of the vehicle, and a complete breakdown of the car's purchase price.

Finance contract or **lease agreement.** This is another legally binding document, listing the terms of the loan or lease—the number of payments, amount of each payment, finance charges, and the responsibilities of the buyer or lessee.

Extended service contract. If you buy one of these, your dealer will register your car with the manufacturer so that you can obtain the services available through the program.

REMEMBER: DON'T SIGN ANYTHING BEFORE READING AND UNDERSTANDING EVERYTHING!

Financing Your Purchase

Unless you are flush with cash, you probably will have to finance all or part of your purchase. That means borrowing money from a bank, the auto manufacturer's finance company, another finance company or credit union, or friends or relatives.

First, you must decide how much you can afford for a down payment and monthly installment payments. Your dealer should be able to help you arrange for a loan and determine monthly payments. If you already have good credit and a relationship with a bank, or if you wish to establish such a relationship, now is a good time to do so.

If you never have had credit in your name (or if your accounts are in your spouse's name), you may need to establish a credit file at your local credit bureau. To do this, ask banks, credit-card companies, and other creditors to file their regular credit reports under both your name and your spouse's name. They are required by law to do this if you ask. This way, you will begin to develop a credit rating.

If you have never before had credit, you may need a co-signer to secure a loan. A co-signer is someone with a good credit rating who agrees to be liable for your loan if for any reason you default on your payments.

Under the federal Truth-in-Lending Act, any financial institution that grants you a loan must provide you with the following information:

Buying a Car

- the price of the product to be purchased;
- the amount of your down payment and any trade-in;
- the balance due;
- the total amount to be financed;
- the total finance charges, expressed in dollars and as an annual percentage rate;
- an itemized list of additional charges;
- the number of payments, their amounts, and due dates;
- the total deferred payment price, including the down payment and all installments;
- any charges for late payments or default;
- the consequences of missed payments;
- a description of any security held by the lender as collateral; and
- a provision for early repayment of the loan.

You may not be familiar with financing terms. Here are a few common ones you should know:

Finance charge: all interest and other charges paid during the term of the loan.

APR: Annual Percentage Rate, a standardized calculation of the interest charges figured on an annual basis.

Add-on interest: A simple method of calculating finance charges on an equal monthly payment contract.

Credit life: A type of insurance that pays off the remaining balance of your loan (or some other specific amount) in the event of your death.

Disability coverage: A type of insurance that pays off your loan (or some other specific amount) if you become disabled. There generally is a waiting period between the time you become disabled and when payments start.

Deferred payment: An installment payment made by mutual agreement at a time later than the original due date.

To Buy or Lease?

An increasing number of individuals and businesses find leasing an attractive alternative to buying. There are several advantages: you usually pay lower monthly charges and can easily trade in for a newer vehicle when the lease period is up. On the other hand, you don't actually own the car, so you usually get nothing when you turn the car back in. Depending on your financial and tax situation, leasing can be a desirable alternative.

Lease arrangements vary widely in duration and mileage and can include insurance or maintenance built into one monthly leasing fee. Among its other advantages, leasing provides simplified record-keeping, which can be convenient at tax time.

Most leasing contracts are for two or three years. There are two types of leases:

Closed-end lease. When the lease is up, you simply turn the car in. You pay nothing unless the car has been damaged or has been driven more miles than you arranged for.

Open-end lease. When the lease is up, you are responsible for the difference in the actual sale price of the vehicle received by the leasing company if it differs from the estimated sale price figured at the beginning of the lease. If the actual sale price is higher than anticipated, you keep the difference; if it's

lower, you make up the difference. Because you are sharing some of the risk, monthly payments generally are lower for this type of lease.

If you decide to lease, the law requires that you be provided with the following information:

- a brief description of the leased property;
- the amount of your deposit at the beginning of the lease;
- the amount of fees, registration, title, or leasing fees or taxes;
- a statement of responsibility if the lease is "open-ended";
- the option to purchase the car, if any;
- your responsibilities at the end of the lease period;
- your servicing and maintenance responsibilities;
- your insurance requirements and responsibilities;
- a description of any security held on the lease;
- the number, amount, and due dates of payments and the total of all payments; and
- the charges and conditions for early termination and charges for delinquent, late payments, or default.

Buying a Car

How to Buy a Used Car

All the same principles apply when buying a used car as when buying a new one. You still need to analyze your needs (with your shopping list of features and options), establish a budget, and gather information. But used cars present a few additional considerations that may help you avoid buying a lot of problems. First and foremost, you must inspect the car very thoroughly. Your inspection should include the exterior, interior, and under the hood.

Exterior. Stand at a distance and look at the paint job to see whether the car has been in an accident. Here's what to check:

Look for ripples in the fenders, dents anywhere, or paint that doesn't match. If the car has been re-painted, it probably has been in an accident.

Look for rust, especially around the bottom of the doors and the rear fenders.

Check the frame for cracks or signs it has been welded. This is another sign of collision damage. If

After you test-drive a used car you are considering buying, check the exhaust tailpipe. A black, sooty deposit may indicate the engine burns oil. A white, powdery deposit usually indicates good fuel combustion.

the frame is bent or damaged badly, you will never get proper use out of the car. It may even be dangerous.

Check under the car for the condition of the muffler, tailpipe, and exhaust system.

Look for signs of fluid leakage on the ground from the engine, transmission, power steering, radiator, brakes, suspension fittings, and shock absorbers.

Walk around the car and check the exterior moldings and window weather-stripping.

Check the condition of all the lenses in all the lights—headlights, tail lights, flashers, back-up lights, brake lights, and turn signals.

Do the shock absorber ''bumper test'' (see page 56). If the car bounces up and down several times, the shocks are worn out.

Open the trunk and check the trunk space. Look for rust and make sure the spare tire is in good condition and that all parts of the jack are present.

Interior. The inside of the car reveals a lot about how well the car was maintained.

Examine the door liners and seat coverings. If the car has seat covers, look under them and check if the upholstery is damaged or dirty. Check the safety belts (make sure *all* of them work), and the headliner.

Make sure all the lights and gauges work.

Have someone stand outside the car while you test the brake to check the brake lights.

Check the odometer mileage. If there is low mileage but the car looks worn and dirty, it's possible the odometer has been tampered with. That, by the way, is a federal offense.

Make sure all the windows crank up and down and that the doors open and lock smoothly.

Under the hood. Here are some things to check:

The condition of belts, hoses, and wires. They shouldn't look cracked or worn.

The battery, to see if it's corroded or cracked.

The fluid levels of all the systems—engine oil, transmission, radiator, brakes, and power steering. If the engine oil is dark and thick, it probably needs changing.

The engine—if it is cleaner than the rest of the car, be suspicious that leaks are being covered up.

Take a test drive. Test-drive the car just as you would a new car. *But be even more cautious.*

Check for too much play in the steering wheel.

Be sensitive to vibrations or noises from the engine, brakes, or steering.

If you hear any noises or feel any vibrations from the transmission, it may need costly repairs.

Test all the accessories—heater, radio, air conditioner, windshield wipers, and so on.

If the car appears to be sluggish, the engine may need an overhaul—another major expense.

Buying a Car

Tires. After the test drive, check the tires. If you felt any vibrations in the steering or a pulling to one side, be suspicious of the tires. Make sure all four tires are the same type and brand and show the same amount of wear.

If at all possible, have a used car checked by a mechanic before you make your final decision. You can have the car thoroughly checked at a diagnostic center for a modest fee. The cost is usually well worth the information. If you find problems (there usually are some, even if they're small ones), it may help you negotiate a better price.

When buying from an individual. The previous owner has a reason for selling the car and it will help to know what it is. The first answer isn't always the real one, so ask as many questions as necessary to get the straight story.

Be careful if the price is too low. It may indicate a problem car.

When buying from a used-car dealer. Do business only with reputable dealers. Check all the local consumer agencies for reports. Most new-car dealers have used-car lots and, because they have full service facilities, can be good places to buy a used car. Some dealers include a warranty with your purchase, usually good for 30 days. Some used cars still have the original manufacturer's warranty, making them excellent values. Make sure you fully understand any warranty.

To recap:
■ Shop the newspapers for prices.
■ Shop the used-car lots.
■ Inspect a used car thoroughly.
■ Go for a test drive.
■ Have the car checked by a mechanic.

One final tip. Establish a $150 to $200 "contingency fund" when you figure the purchase price of a used car. You'll inevitably have to spend this money for some minor repairs.

Chapter Five

How to Sell a Car

How to Sell a Car

When you decide to get a new car, the question always comes up: What do you do with your old car? Most new-car buyers trade it in to the new-car dealer; it's generally quicker, easier, and more convenient. But it also can be costlier. You almost always can get more money by selling your car privately, usually through a classified ad or by word of mouth.

If you still owe money on the loan for your car (or for any other loan for which you've used your car as security), there should be no problem, as long as you pay the lender "off the top" of the money you get from the sale. In some cases, the purchaser may want to assume the loan, if it's assumable. By visiting the lending institution with the prospective buyer, you can conclude the transaction with a minimum of red tape.

How do you determine whether to trade in or sell? First, you must calculate the true trade-in value of your car. Then, you must determine its fair market resale value (the amount you can reasonably expect to get by selling it yourself).

As discussed in Chapter Four, some car dealers will be generous with the trade-in value of your car, but give you little or no discount on the purchase price of your new car. Other dealers will be stingy on the trade-in allowance, but generous on the new-car discount. The only way to determine the true value of the old car is to ask the dealer to quote a price both with and without a trade-in.

There are several ways to find out how much you could get by selling the car yourself. First and foremost, check the used-car section of the classifieds to find the asking prices of cars similar to yours in make, model, and age. Another source is the *Official Used Car Price Guide*, also known as the "Blue Book," available from any car dealer or bank loan officer. Other versions are available at bookstores and newsstands.

Keep in mind the general condition of your car and the number of miles on its odometer. If you have taken good care of your car and it looks fine and runs fine, you can expect top dollar. People generally are willing to pay substantially more for a well-maintained vehicle. It will help to show your well-kept maintenance and repair records, proving you kept the car in good working condition. (Of course, if your car is in top condition, you should be questioning why you're selling it in the first place. Conversely, if your car is in terrible condition, you may have a difficult time finding a buyer at any price.)

Whether trading in or selling privately, outward appearance is very important. The more effort the buyer (whether a dealer or individual) must put into your car to make it presentable, the less it will be worth. Before selling or trading in, clean the engine, the interior, and the exterior. Those three items, which cost less than $50 (for the engine cleaning and a good professional wax job), could bring in hundreds of extra dollars. They even could mean the difference between making a sale and not making a sale.

Make sure all obvious minor mechanical problems are corrected. A burned-out turn-signal bulb or a malfunctioning radio indicates a lack of attention that could turn off a prospective buyer.

Let's review the four main steps:
- ■ Determine the true market value of your car.
- ■ Determine its real trade-in allowance.
- ■ Make sure the car is clean and presentable.
- ■ Correct any minor defects and get it into good operating condition.

Selling a Car

Making the Sale

So you've decided to sell the car yourself. Now you must decide what you want for the car and establish the lowest price acceptable. You already have checked with the new-car dealer and determined what you can expect on a trade-in. A good "bottom-line" figure might be $300 above the trade-in allowance, to justify your extra time, effort, and costs.

Buy an inexpensive "FOR SALE" sign at a five-and-dime or hardware store. Place it in a side window with your phone number in large, legible print. You also might add some basic information, such as year, make, and model. You probably shouldn't list your asking price. Try to park the car in the most visible spot possible. Perhaps a friendly local service station will let you park it there on weekends.

Next, work up an ad for your local newspaper with all the pertinent information. A typical ad might read:

'79 Ford 4 dr. LTD, fully equipped, 1 owner, low miles, ex. cond., must sell, $4395. 555-2638 after 6 p.m.

You will be charged for the number of characters or lines in the ad, so abbreviate whenever possible. Shoppers generally are looking for a car in a narrow year/model/price range, so great detail isn't necessary.

A few additional tips on running an ad:
■ The best time to run an ad is on weekends.
■ Let your friends, relatives, and co-workers know the car is for sale. They may know someone—or may be interested themselves.
■ Post index cards with the pertinent information on community bulletin boards at grocery stores, community centers, apartment buildings, or other appropriate places. They're a good source of free advertising.

When you get a call about the car, have as much information on hand as possible. Know the exact mileage and be sure to point out its best features.

Here are some other suggestions to help make a sale:
■ If the car generally is parked in a garage and not outside, point that out.

■ If you have records of the car's maintenance history, that's another excellent selling point.

■ If you have established a price that might be considered to be on the high side, explain that the car is worth it and you'd be willing to discuss it further if a potential buyer comes over to take a look.

■ Try hard to get prospective buyers to see the car. If one of them knows the price and can be persuaded to take a test drive, chances are you've made a sale.

■ Be ready to make adjustments in your price if someone is interested but not yet sold. A minor drop in price may be all that's needed to make a sale.

A word of caution: If you live alone, it's a good idea when screening phone callers to allude to a father, brother, husband, or neighbor if you are suspicious of the caller's intentions.

Selling a Car

Chapter Six

Trouble on the Road

Trouble on the Road

We drive thousands of miles every year. If we're lucky, those miles are trouble-free. Whether it happens or not, however, the anxiety of a car breakdown is often there.

What to Do if Your Car Dies

You're driving along, minding your own business. Suddenly, the car sputters, slows down, and stops running.

What do you do? First, don't panic.

Next, take action:

■ If the car is still rolling, it's important to use that momentum to get the car off the road as safely and as quickly as possible, particularly if you're on a highway. Put your emergency flashers on, put the car in neutral, and ease off as far to the right as possible. On a divided highway, if you're in the far left lane, you may have to pull off to the left, if there is a shoulder to use. Ideally, though, always try to pull off to the right.

■ After you're safely off the road, check the traffic to get safely out of the car. Use the passenger door, if possible.

■ Raise the hood and tie a white cloth or handkerchief to the antenna or door handle to signal an emergency.

■ If it's night, it is best to stay in your car—with doors locked and windows up—until help arrives. If you do leave your car to make a phone call, make sure you know exactly where you've parked so you can explain it accurately to whomever you call. Look for landmarks you can describe to someone. Most highways have mileage markers that make excellent landmarks.

Here are some things you can do that may enable you to drive safely off the road and get to a service station:

■ Check the fuel gauge. It's easy to forget your gas tank—your ''breakdown'' could be something as simple as running out of gas.

■ Raise the hood and check for loose wires. Look especially at the wires going from the distributor to the sparkplugs and from the coil to the distributor. Check the battery connections to see if they are loose.

■ Try your lights, horn, and radio to see if your electrical system is working. If they work, however, it doesn't neccessarily mean the electrical system is okay. But if they don't work, you know you've got an electrical problem.

■ If the motor turns over when you attempt to restart it, and you didn't notice any obvious loose wires, it could be a fuel problem such as a vapor lock, which generally occurs in hot weather. This often will correct itself if you let the car cool for about ten or fifteen minutes and then restart it. If it restarts, drive to the nearest service station and ask a mechanic to check the fuel system.

Flat tire. If you have a flat tire or, even worse, a blowout, slow down immediately. Look for a safe, flat (preferably hard) surface on which you can change a tire. If you are close to a service station, you may be able to drive a few hundred yards on a flat tire—but don't drive very far on a blowout. Expect the steering wheel to vibrate, so hold on tightly and concentrate. Put your emergency blinkers on. If the blowout is in the front, the car will dart to the side of the blowout. If it's in the rear, you can expect some back-and forth movement known as ''fishtailing.'' See page 114 for ''How to Change a Flat Tire.''

Brake failure. If your brakes fail (a spongy brake pedal is a common warning), first try pumping the pedal. If this doesn't increase the pedal pressure, immediately downshift into the lowest gear possible. Then, gently

How to Change a Flat Tire

1. If you get a flat tire while driving, pull off to the right as far as possible, on a flat, hard surface.

2. Put the car in "park" and put on the emergency brake.

3. Anchor the wheel on the *opposite corner* to the flat tire, using a rock or block of wood. (If the right rear tire is flat, for example, put the anchor under the left front tire.)

4. Remove the jack, lug wrench, and related items from your trunk, and get your screwdriver from your tool kit.

5. Use the screwdriver to remove the wheel cover from the wheel.

6. Using the lug wrench, *loosen* each of the lug nuts. (Don't remove them yet.) It may be difficult to start some of the nuts, so use a little ingenuity. For example, step on the lug wrench, or use a heavy object like a hammer to force the nut loose.

7. Position the jack securely under the car according to the instructions in your owner's manual. Jack up the car so the wheel you need to change is about two to three inches off the ground.

Bumper Jack
(larger cars)

8. Remove the lug nuts. It's a good idea to put them inside a wheel cover so you won't lose them.

9. Remove the flat tire and roll it out of your way.

10. Put the new tire on and tighten the lug nuts by hand so the wheel is securely attached to the bolts. Be careful not to jar the car (you could knock it off the jack).

11. Lower the car until the tire is just touching the ground and cannot freely turn. Then, tighten the lug nuts with the wrench until they are evenly tightened. When you tighten them, work diagonally: tighten one on top, then one on the bottom, then one on the left, then the right, and so on.

12. Lower the car completely and give the lug nuts a final tightening.

13. Put everything back into the trunk. Leave the wheel cover off to remind you that, after it's fixed, the original tire should go back onto the car.

Scissors Jack
(smaller cars)

but firmly apply your parking or emergency brake. Be careful: If you apply it too abruptly, the car could go into a skid.

Headlight failure. If your headlights go out suddenly, try using your parking lights or directional signals to see sufficiently to drive to a safe place. If you're on a well-lighted road, you should have no problem, but keep your other lights on so approaching cars can see you. If this happens on a dark road, use a flashlight (you should always have one in your glove compartment or toolbox) to guide you to a safe spot. Open your window and shine it as far ahead as possible.

Breakdowns at night. If you have any breakdown at night, try to park under a street light or other well-lighted area.

Windshield wipers. If your windshield wipers fail in a heavy rainstorm, roll down your window and look out the side so you can see far enough ahead to get to a safe spot.

> *It's good to know how many miles your car can travel on a tank of gas. If you always set your dashboard "trip meter" to zero when filling up, you'll have a good idea of how many more miles you can go when you're running low.*

Stopping on the highway. If you must pull off onto the shoulder of a highway, be sure to park on something solid enough for the wheels to grip. Otherwise, you'll have no traction when you want to drive away, and you may get stuck. If you do get stuck, things like branches, sand, gravel, and cinders work well to get you moving. Place them under the *rear* wheels (if you have a front-wheel-drive car, use the *front* wheels) and cover the ground both in front of and behind the wheels.

When you start to pull away, it may help to use a higher gear. This reduces wheel spin. If the wheels do spin, it may help to rock the car back and forth by going a few inches forward, then a few inches back.

Bad-Weather Driving Tips

■ Use your turn signals well in advance of making any movements.

■ Use extra care in applying smooth movement to the accelerator pedal and brake pedal, and when turning the steering wheel.

■ Avoid using brakes unnecessarily by increasing the distance between your car and others and by anticipating the need to slow down. When you need to slow down or stop, remove your foot from the accelerator and allow the engine drag to slow the car down. (With a manual transmission, you can downshift into the next lowest gear.)

■ On a snowy road, stay in the "groove" of a cleared highway or follow other tire tracks. Always avoid driving through unplowed snow.

■ In fog, heavy rain, or snow: Use your regular lights, not your high beams; bright lights can reflect back at you, decreasing your visibility. If you have trouble seeing, switch to high beams briefly to get a glance of conditions ahead.

■ If visibility is limited, slow down to a comfortable speed, but try to keep moving at a steady pace. If you are traveling more slowly than the rest of the traffic, consider turning on your emergency flasher lights.

■ If you must stop, select a spot where you can get clear of traffic flow. Use your turn signal well in advance of turning off, and leave your emergency flashers on while stopped. If available, an overpass can provide some temporary relief from the elements and may allow you to be better seen by others.

You accomplish this by changing gears from forward to reverse in a rhythmic manner. But don't do this for long; it's very hard on your transmission.

Seeing the Light

From time to time, your warning lights or gauges will indicate a problem with your fuel, electrical, or lubrication systems. Here's what you should do:

Alternator light. This means your battery no longer is being charged, but you can still drive for a while on your battery's reserve power. At night, however, your headlights will be dimmer than normal, so stay on well-lighted routes. Because your battery supplies power to all electrical devices, you should turn off ones you can temporarily do without—the air conditioner, for example, or the heater or radio. Then go to the nearest service station to have your alternator and battery checked. The problem may be that your battery no longer is capable of holding a charge. If so, you'll have to get it replaced. The problem also could be fan belts that need tightening or a malfunctioning alternator.

Your Emergency Tool Kit

The more you travel, the more important it is to have a complete selection of emergency tools in your car. Here are some things you should keep in your car at all times in case you have trouble on the road:

Electrician's tape	Jumper cables
Empty gas can	Phillips-head
Fire extinguisher	screwdrivers
Flares	Pliers
Flashlight	Reflectors
Flat-head	Rope
screwdrivers	White rags

Temperature light. This tells you the radiator coolant is overheating or you've lost water from your radiator and the engine is getting too hot. This typically happens while driving in heavy traffic, in hot weather, with your air conditioner on. The first thing you should do is turn off your air conditioner. If the light stays on, turn on your heater. This sounds strange,

How to Jump-Start a Car

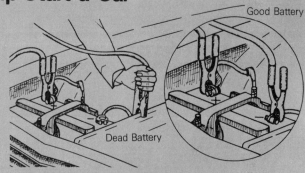

Good Battery

Dead Battery

■ Position the other car so that its battery is as close as possible to your battery.

■ Turn the power off in both cars. Put them both in park and set the parking brakes.

■ Connect the clamps of the red cable to the positive posts of each battery. The positive posts are marked either ''POS'' or '' + .'' Be careful not to let the metal clamps of the red and black cables touch each other at any time.

■ *On the car with the good battery:* connect one end of the black cable to the negative post (marked either ''NEG'' or ''—.'' *On the car with the dead battery:* connect the black cable to bare metal on the car's frame. This acts as a ground connection. Be careful the cable isn't near the fan or fan belt, or it could get tangled when your car starts.

■ Check to make sure the ignition is off in the car with the dead battery; then start up the car with

the good battery. Rev the engine a little to insure the battery is charged.

■ Start the car with the dead battery.

■ With both cars running, disconnect the cables, starting with the ground connection (the black cable attached to the bare metal), then the other black cable, and finally the two red cables.

■ Keep your engine running until you get help or reach your final destination.

and it may be uncomfortable, but it will draw heat away from the engine—and blow it inside the car.

If this still doesn't help, stop your car in a safe place, shift your transmission into neutral, and rev your engine by stepping on the gas for a second. The revving helps the engine fan cool the radiator. Next, turn the engine off and let everything cool down. It will take anywhere from ten minutes to a half hour, depending on the outside temperature and how hot the engine actually got. It will help to open the hood to release the heat. Then check to see whether a radiator hose has come loose, has a hole or crack, or has broken completely.

You'll also need to check the water/coolant level in the radiator by unscrewing the cap slightly, then completely removing it. **Warning:** *Never remove the radiator cap when the engine is hot. You can be seriously burned.* If you need to add water or coolant, do so when the engine is running.

Oil light. The oil light sometimes will flicker while you're stopped in traffic. That could mean one of two things: your engine is idling too slowly or your oil level is low. If the red light stays on, you could be losing oil pressure. *You should go immediately to a service station. Otherwise, you risk serious engine damage.*

Chapter Seven

Driving Like a Pro

Driving Like a Pro

Driving is a very demanding skill, both mentally and physically. It requires good reflexes, good judgment, and good will toward other motorists. Perhaps because we do it so often, I think we tend to take driving for granted. We drive ''automatically'' until something goes wrong; then our reflexes are too slow to react appropriately and safely.

Driving safely in a city or on a highway is not very different from driving safely on a race track, except that it's usually at a much slower speed. (I sometimes feel it's safer on the race track, because at least everyone is traveling in the same direction.) Both types of driving depend largely on your ability to cope with rapidly changing traffic situations.

Insurance industry statistics show that the vast majority of accidents happen on good roads in daylight and involve cars with no apparent defects. The greatest single cause of accidents is the driver.

The reasons for accidents vary. In one accident, the problem may be a lack of driving skills or experience. In another, it may be a momentary lapse of attention (talking to a passenger, looking at the scenery, or daydreaming, for example). Other accidents might be caused by a failure to compensate for bad road conditions, driving while impaired by alcohol or drugs, fatigue, or simple overconfidence. Fortunately, all these problems can be corrected.

Anyone can learn to drive. But learning to drive *well* is a different matter. Driving excellence calls for constant effort and practice—and concentration at *all* times.

It's extremely important that when you get into your car, before you drive away, you are properly seated. For example:

■ You should sit so your body fits firmly against the seat back and cushion.

■ You should sit as upright as possible (it helps you stay alert).

■ Your arms should be slightly bent—approximately at a 120-degree to 140-degree angle.

■ Your hands should grip the wheel lightly but firmly in the "ten o'clock" and "two o'clock" positions. This gives you excellent car control.

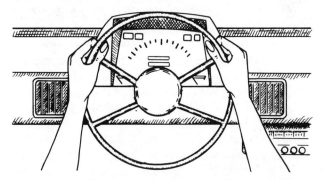

This position gives you excellent car control.

■ Your feet should reach the pedals easily, with a slight bend in your legs. Never have your legs so straight that you must stretch to work the pedals with the tips of your toes. Your seat should be forward enough so that when the brakes or clutch are fully

depressed, your knees still are slightly bent. To check, place your right foot flat on the floor under the brake pedal. If you can do this without stretching, you're positioned properly.

After you've properly positioned the seat, then adjust the mirrors. Mirrors are a very important driving aid. To use them effectively, your side mirrors should be positioned so you can see the rear quarter panel on the inside edge of the mirror and the ground on the bottom edge; your rear-view mirror should be positioned to provide maximum visibility through the rear window.

The last adjustment is the most important: **your seat belt.** I can't say enough to encourage the use of seat belts. Not only should the driver use them, so should all passengers. After personally experiencing several racing accidents, watching the 31-mile-per-hour crash test at the Ford Motor Company testing grounds, and talking with enough accident victims (both with and without seat belts), I have no doubts that seat belts work and save lives. I enjoy living too much to take the chance and not wear them. Here's a tip on how to incorporate the seat-belt habit into your life: If you do it twelve times in a row, it will become a habit. So do it!

The Two-Second Rule

One of the most common driver errors is following another vehicle too closely, often called "tailgating." Here is a simple "two-second rule" to estimate your following distance and to properly judge a safe distance:

■ Wait until the car ahead approaches a "checkpoint" like a road sign or telephone pole.
■ Begin counting as the rear of the car ahead passes the checkpoint. Count seconds: "one thousand one, one thousand two . . ."
■ Stop counting as the front of your car reaches the checkpoint.
■ If it took two seconds or more to reach the checkpoint, your following distance is safe; if it was less than two seconds, you're tailgating.

Driving with Vision

Driving in traffic takes concentration. In fact, you

Fastening seat belts (for you and your passengers) should become part of your routine every time you get in a car. I've been told that if you do something twelve times in a row it will become habit. So start counting.

should have little time for anything else—even casual conversation with passengers. Some of my friends don't like driving with me because I don't talk much when I drive. That's because I'm concentrating on my driving. I do it because I like to drive and I like to know I'm in total control of the vehicle.

Because there is so much to watch for and attend to, it's important that you view traffic selectively, paying close attention to those matters that concern you the most. Your most important tools are your eyes.

The key to accident-free driving can be summarized in five rules:

1. Look up and ahead. How far ahead you can look depends a lot on the density of the traffic. On a

There's no truth to the rumor that pregnant women shouldn't wear seat belts. According to the American Medical Association, "both the pregnant mother and the fetus are safer, provided the lap belt is worn as low on the pelvis as possible."

highway, you should look far ahead and let your peripheral vision take care of what's up close. You needn't worry about missing situations close by—your brain won't let you. It will attract you automatically to nearby situations that demand your immediate attention.

But don't simply stare straight ahead. To see properly, your eyes must move constantly, always focusing immediately on whatever they see. One of the keys to winning races at 200 miles per hour is being able to focus instantly on the field in front of you. Even at 55 miles per hour, you increase safety and driving enjoyment if you can look ahead.

Here's a simple exercise you can do on the highway to practice and develop your "eye lead time." You should try this as a front-seat passenger—not while you're driving:

■ Look straight ahead, down the road, as you usually do while driving.
■ Locate a telephone pole about a quarter of a mile away.
■ Practice moving your eyes (but not your head) back and forth from straight ahead to the telephone pole, focusing for a moment in each direction—to the right and to the left.
■ As the car moves down the road, move your focus to the next telephone pole, and the next one, and on and on. But don't forget to keep moving your eyes back to look straight ahead—after all, you're supposed to be "driving."

The more you practice, the more times you'll be able to move your eyes back and forth from the road to each telephone pole, focusing on each. When you really do drive, this technique helps you to scan the road constantly, keeping alert to all that is going on. A good rule of thumb is to be aware of traffic condi-

> *When checking your mirrors, both side and rear-view, include a glance at the dashboard gauges to make sure everything is running okay. If you get into this habit, you'll be in constant touch with potential problems on the road and in your car.*

tions at least eight seconds of driving time down the road.

2. Look behind. Good drivers develop a systematic routine for looking ahead, from side-to-side—and into the rear-view mirror. In fact, you should check your mirrors every five to ten seconds, and always before you stop, turn, or change lanes.

Even if your mirrors are correctly positioned, there still is a "blind spot" on each side of the car. Make sure other drivers aren't driving in your blind spot. And, to help other motorists, don't drive in their blind spots. It's a good driving practice to glance over your shoulder, as well as into the mirror, before you change lanes. Develop your own routine: mirror, signal, shoulder glance, lane change. When stopping, check your mirror as you brake. This can prevent accidents, or at least prepare you for someone approaching too fast from behind.

Some side-view mirrors have a curved glass. This convex lens increases the range of vision, but objects seen in the mirror actually are closer than they appear. You must accommodate for the difference.

3. Get the big picture. The "big picture" is sidewalk to sidewalk and extends from your front bumper to a full city block ahead (a half-mile ahead on rural roads). Look ahead and watch for people in parked cars as well as pedestrians, and watch especially for children and bicyclists. Keep track of what's going on behind you, too.

4. Anticipate everything. Besides having good reflexes and eyesight, you should anticipate everything that might happen. Anticipate trouble ahead; assume the worst conditions and allow for every possible error. I always watch the front wheels of the cars next to me on a highway. I can see them start to turn before they actually turn the car. I then can anticipate their moves and alter my position accordingly.

5. Be seen. Make sure other drivers see you. Visual contact with other drivers at intersections is essential. Drivers don't intentionally drive into other vehicles—they simply don't see them. So, be sure you see them, and that they see you. Don't hesitate to use your horn or headlights to establish eye-to-eye contact.

Driving at Night

Night driving is difficult. But there are things you can do to minimize the difficulty. Always keep your headlights and windshield clean and your washers full of fluid.

When meeting oncoming cars with bright headlights, it is hard to adjust your eyes to the glare because your eyes often are drawn to the bright lights. This is something I learned while driving en-

Indecision behind the wheel can be extremely dangerous. Concentrate on what you're doing and try to decide what you'll do before you do it. Anticipate as much as possible.

durance races, like "12 Hours of Sebring" and "24 Hours of Daytona," two top racing events. There, the headlights are extremely intense, yet I find myself almost drawn to the other cars' lights. It takes some discipline, but you have to resist the urge to look at the lights. Instead, *look up and straight ahead* beyond the lights and slightly to the right or left. On the highway, you need to switch to low-beam lights when you are within 500 feet of oncoming traffic. Use your low beams when following another car within about 200 feet. On country roads, lower your headlights when approaching the crest of a hill or a sharp turn. If there are no headlights visible, switch back to the high beams for better visibility. When passing other cars at night, it's a good idea to flash your high beams to warn the driver you wish to pass.

Driving Tips

Safe Braking

Under normal conditions, you anticipate stops by braking early, bringing the car to a stop smoothly and safely. You should always use your right foot—not your left—on the brake.

In bad weather, braking requires a gradual application of the brakes to avoid locking the wheels on wet, icy, or snow-covered roads. If you do go into a skid from locking brakes, remember this: It's almost impossible to brake and steer at the same time. So ease up on the brakes slightly until the wheels unlock, and then reapply pressure on the brake pedal to bring the car to a stop. If you are braking and then decide to turn, first take your foot off the brake pedal. But keep

Try to avoid short trips. They are expensive because they usually involve a "cold" engine. For the first mile or two a cold engine gets only 30 percent to 40 percent of the mileage it gets after it's warmed up.

in mind that the vehicle will travel in the direction the wheels are turned.

If you do get into a skid, turn the steering wheel in the direction of the skid. If the rear of the car is skidding to the right, for example, turn the wheel to the right. If you steer in the opposite direction, the car may go into a spin. You need to gain control of the direction of the car. Slow it down and either bring it to a stop or steer it in a safe direction.

Driving for Fuel Economy

When you drive safely, you also usually get maximum fuel economy. In general, good fuel economy comes from driving smoothly at moderate speeds and light acceleration. Here are some tips for getting the most miles per gallon:
- Accelerate gently and smoothly. Avoid "jackrabbit" starts.
- Anticipate stops. Leave space for gradual braking.
- Practice gentle "footwork" on the gas pedal. Maintain a constant rate of speed if possible.
- Drive in the proper gear. Use the highest gear possible, but when the engine "lugs" (a sort of

> *Carry a tire gauge in your glove compart-*
> *ment. Many service stations (especially*
> *self-service stations) don't have them.*

pulsating, jerky motion), shift to the next lower gear.

■ Use your air conditioner only when necessary.

■ Avoid idling for long periods.

■ Drive at optimum speeds. On compact and sub-compact cars, fuel economy peaks at about 40 mph. As a result, your fuel economy will be about the same at 45 mph as at 30 mph. On larger cars, top fuel economy is at about 45 mph.

■ Minimize the amount of weight you carry. The extra weight (and the wind resistance, if you carry things on a roof luggage rack) reduce your gas mileage.

■ Keep your car well tuned.

■ Keep the air pressure in your tires at the maximum recommended by the manufacturer (or even slightly higher — see page 59).

Concentrate, anticipate, and be smooth with all movements in the car and you will be a safer, more economical driver. And you will reap the benefits in safety and enjoyment.

Driving Tips

Troubleshooting

What Your Car Is Trying to Tell You

ENGINE RESPONSE

CUTS OUT (either a temporary but complete loss of power or the engine quits at sharp, irregular intervals, usually under heavy acceleration).
Answer: This could mean the engine is occasionally receiving the wrong amount of fuel or the ignition system is arbitrarily turning itself off and on. Check the carburetor, fuel pump, fuel filter, and ignition spark.

HESITATES (momentarily under acceleration—it can happen at any speed, but usually occurs during a stop, sometimes causing the engine to stall).
Answer: The air/fuel mixture is out of adjustment. Check the carburetor.

MISSES (pulses or jerks, usually with changes in engine speed—not normally felt around 30 mph).
Answer: Check sparkplugs or sparkplug wires for wear or corrosion.

IDLES ROUGH (engine runs unevenly and shakes).
Answer: Poor idle adjustment, dirty air filter or PCV valve, pinched vacuum hose, or worn engine parts. Start with simple adjustments before undertaking more difficult tasks.

What Your Car Is Trying to Tell You

HANDLING PROBLEMS

BRAKE FADES (stopping action seems to decrease).
Answer: Brake fluid may be overheating from long, hard use. Try pumping brakes rather than stepping on them hard.

BRAKE PEDAL IS LOW (you have to push down far to engage the brakes).
Answer: Worn or poorly adjusted brake linings or pads or a leak in the lines. Have the brakes inspected as soon as possible.

BRAKES PULL OR GRAB (car tends to move to one side when you brake, or brakes engage suddenly when applying normal pressure).
Answer: Brakes need adjusting. Have them inspected as soon as possible.

EXCESSIVE PLAY IN THE STEERING WHEEL (you must turn the wheel more than usual before the car responds).
Answer: Steering components need adjustment.

STEERING IS DIFFICULT (the car is extremely difficult to turn, especially during parking).
Answer: Possible low power-steering fluid. If not, have the steering linkage checked.

What Your Car Is Trying to Tell You

CAR PULLS TO ONE SIDE (when steering straight).
Answer: Check the tire pressure; one tire could be low. If not, have the front-end alignment checked.

WHEEL SHIMMIES (a rapid side-to-side motion in the steering wheel, especially at high speeds).
Answer: Probable loose steering linkage or wheels out of balance.

VIBRATION (the whole car shakes, usually at a specific speed).
Answer: Could be out-of-balance wheels or poorly tuned engine.

WANDERS (requires frequent steering correction to maintain direction).
Answer: Could need wheel alignment or steering adjustment.

SWAYS OR PITCHES (car takes a long time to recover from bumps).
Answer: Check shock absorbers.

BOTTOMS (you feel a heavy thud when going over a bump).
Answer: The car is bouncing too much. Replace the shock absorbers.

Troubleshooting Checklist

Noise	Likely Solution
Pings and knocks	Higher octane fuel, timing adjustment, tune-up
Squealing during braking	Brake linings are worn and need replacing
Clicking from engine	Low pressure. Check oil level and oil pump
Engine run-on after turning off ignition	Idle speed or timing need adjustment
Popping from exhaust	Fouled sparkplugs or faulty ignition wires need replacing
Popping or roar during acceleration	Check exhaust system for damage
High-pitched screech during acceleration	Check for loose fan belt; it may need replacing
Squealing tires	Increase tire pressure
Coughing or sputtering	Engine is not getting the proper amount of fuel; check for possible clogged fuel filter, faulty fuel pump, or stuck choke
Clanking while traveling on a rough road	Check shock absorbers for excessive wear
Hissing from the engine	Check for loss of coolant or loose radiator hose

How to Spot Trouble

Visual Sign	Likely Solution
Green fluid	Radiator coolant is leaking: check hoses and radiator
Brown fluid	Engine oil is leaking; check for faulty seals, fittings, or gaskets
Red fluid	Transmission or power-steering fluid is leaking; check for faulty seals or gaskets
Black grease	Check rear axles for leaks

Maintenance Checklist

Maintenance Schedule

EVERY TIME YOU GET GAS OR ONCE A WEEK	EVERY 4,000 MILES OR THREE TIMES A YEAR	EVERY 12,000 MILES OR ONCE A YEAR
ELECTRICAL SYSTEM • check water level in battery • check windshield-washer fluid	• clean battery terminals • check all lightbulbs, lenses • check sparkplug wires • inspect windshield-wiper blades	• replace condenser • replace distributor cap • replace rotor • change sparkplugs • check freon in air conditioner
FUEL SYSTEM • add fuel	• check air filter (change if necessary)	• change air filter • change fuel filter • replace PCV valve
EXHAUST SYSTEM	• Inspect muffler, exhaust pipe, tailpipe	• all 4,000-mile items

Maint. Checklist

Maintenance Schedule

EVERY TIME YOU GET GAS OR ONCE A WEEK	EVERY 4,000 MILES OR THREE TIMES A YEAR	EVERY 12,000 MILES OR ONCE A YEAR
TRANSMISSION SYSTEM • check fluid	• check fluid level • check clutch linkage/travel	• change filter • inspect linkage • all 4,000-mile items
ENGINE LUBRICATION SYSTEM • check oil level	• change oil • change oil filter	• all 4,000-mile items
COOLING SYSTEM • check water level in radiator	• check belts • check radiator hoses • check radiator cap • check water pump	• drain and flush radiator • all 4,000-mile items

Maintenance Schedule

EVERY TIME YOU GET GAS OR ONCE A WEEK	EVERY 4,000 MILES OR THREE TIMES A YEAR	EVERY 12,000 MILES OR ONCE A YEAR
BRAKE SYSTEM • check brake fluid	• check brake fluid level • adjust parking brake • check brake pedal height • check brake pads/shoes	• all 4,000-mile items • change brake fluid
STEERING SYSTEM • check power steering fluid	• check ball joints • check grease fittings • check steering linkage	• all 4,000-mile items • lubricate front wheel bearings
SUSPENSION SYSTEM		• replace shock absorbers if necessary
TIRES & WHEELS • check air pressure	• check tire wear • check alignment	• all 4,000-mile items

Maint. Checklist

141

Sample Maintenance Checklist

Mileage	Fuel (gal.)	MPG	Oil (qt.)	Water	ATF	Power Steering Fluid	Wind- shield Fluid	Brake Fluid	Tire Pressure				Cost (dol.)
									LF	RF	LR	RR	

Glossary

Accelerator. Also known as the "gas pedal," it controls the amount of fuel you send to the carburetor.

Aerodynamics. The science of designing car shapes to travel with the least air resistance. The less resistance, the less fuel is required to move the car. Automobile designers use an index called a "drag coefficient" to measure aerodynamics.

Air filter/cleaner. A filter located near the carburetor that removes dirt from the air before it is mixed with fuel and sent into the engine.

Alternator. This uses the movement of the engine to generate electricity to keep the battery charged.

Anti-sway bar. See **Stabilizer bar.**

ATF filter. A filter in the automatic transmission fluid container that helps keep the fluid free from dirt.

Automatic transmission fluid (ATF). An oil that lubricates and cools the components in the automatic transmission.

Battery. It stores electrical energy used to start the car and to power all its electrical accessories.

Booster cables. A pair of heavy wires with clamps on each end used to transfer electrical power from a charged battery to a dead one. These must be used with care, or you could damage your car or injure yourself. They also are known as "jumper cables."

Brake calipers. The housing for the brake pads on disc brakes. When you step on the brake, the calipers force the brake pads against the discs, creating friction that slows or stops the car.

Brake fluid. A special fluid you put into the master cylinder. The fluid travels down brake lines every time you step on the brake pedal.

Brake line. Hoses and tubes that carry the brake fluid from the master cylinder to each wheel.

Brake pad. A flat metal piece on disc brakes. When you step on the brake pedal, the pad presses against the brake disc to slow or stop the car.

Glossary

Brake shoe. A curved metal piece on drum brakes. When you step on the brake pedal, the shoe presses against the inside of the drum to slow or stop the car.

Bubbleback. A car designed with a large, rounded back window.

Camber. The measurement of how far the front wheels angle in or out at the top. Proper camber helps to ensure maximum tire life. The exact adjustment is different for every car.

Camshaft. A shaft located near the top of the engine. Connected to it are rods that open and close the valves that let air and fuel into each cylinder. The rods also open valves that let exhaust fumes escape.

Carburetor. The meeting place for air and fuel. The carburetor mixes the two to produce a vapor, which is exploded in each cylinder.

Caster. An adjustment that helps the front wheels swing back to the straight-ahead position after you complete a turn.

Catalytic converter. An emission-control device that extracts unburned hydrocarbons from exhaust gases.

Chassis. The basic structure of an automobile, including the frame, axles, and suspension system—everything except the engine and the outside body.

Choke. An automatic valve that enriches the air/fuel mixture to help your car start when the engine is cold.

Circuit breaker. A switch or relay for breaking an electrical circuit if there are abnormalities in the current flow.

Clutch. This links the transmission to the engine in cars with manual transmission. When you step on the clutch pedal, it disconnects the engine from the transmission and allows you to shift from one gear to another.

Coil. A transformer that boosts your battery's twelve volts into the more than 15,000 volts needed to turn over the engine.

Coil spring. A type of spring used in the suspension system.

Combustion chamber. The space inside each cylinder where the air/fuel mixture is exploded.

Condenser. An electrical device located in the distributor that helps prevent ''arcing'' at the points, which can reduce fuel efficiency. Cars with electronic ignition systems don't have these.

Control Arm. A metal rod in the suspension system that allows the front wheels to move up and down when going over bumps.

Coolant. The mixture of antifreeze and water that is stored in the radiator.

Crankcase. A section at the bottom of the engine that contains the crankshaft, oil pump, oil pan, and engine oil.

Crankshaft. A shaft located in the base of the engine that is connected to each piston. The crankshaft

transports the energy created by the pistons to the transmission.

Cylinder. The space inside the engine where each piston moves up and down. Most cars have from four to eight cylinders (although a few have as many as twelve cylinders). Common configurations are ''V-6'' and ''V-8,'' in which there are six or eight cylinders and their layout resembles the letter ''V''; a ''straight-6'' engine has six cylinders all in a single row.

Diesel engine. A high-compression engine designed to burn diesel fuel. Diesel engines do not have spark-plugs.

Diesel fuel. A low-grade kerosene fuel used to power diesel engines.

Differential. A gearbox connected to the driveshaft, which carries the power to the driving wheels.

Dipstick. A small rod used to measure levels of fluid, such as engine oil and automatic transmission fluid.

Glossary

Markings on the dipstick indicate whether the fluid level is adequate.

Disc brakes. A braking system using metal discs that turn with the wheels. Pads squeeze each disc when you step on the brake pedal.

Distributor. The part of the engine's electrical system that directs electrical current to each sparkplug at the precise moment required and in the correct sequence.

Distributor cap. This protects the distributor from moisture and dirt.

Driveshaft. A shaft that transmits the power from the transmission to the rear axle in rear-wheel-drive cars. (In front-wheel-drive cars, it is incorporated into the transaxle.)

Drivetrain. The collective name of the engine, transmission, driveshaft, and axles.

Drum brakes. A braking system using metal drums mounted to the axles. Brake shoes press against the inside of the drums when you step on the brake pedal.

Engine block. The main part of the engine; contains the cylinders, pistons, and other major moving parts.

Engine "knock." A clattering noise from the engine caused by improperly burned fuel.

EPA rating. An estimate of fuel economy from the U.S. Environmental Protection Agency. EPA ratings are developed from standardized laboratory tests, so they may not reflect actual driving experience.

Exhaust pipe. This carries gases created by the exploded air/fuel mixture from the exhaust manifold, through the catalytic converter and the muffler, then out into the atmosphere.

Fan. It draws air through the radiator to lower the coolant temperature.

Flooding. The result of too much fuel pumped into the engine from the carburetor, often occurring when starting the car. When it happens, turn off the ignition and let the car sit for at least a minute before trying to start it again. You can eliminate most flooding problems by following the manufacturer's recommendations for starting contained in your owner's manual.

Flywheel. A large circular gear attached to the crankshaft, which engages when you start the engine.

Four-wheel drive. A transmission system in which all four wheels are controlled by the transmission, as opposed to just the front wheels or rear wheels. This system provides better handling on roads covered with rain, snow, and ice.

Front-wheel drive. A transmission system in which the front wheels provide the driving power. (Most cars have rear-wheel drive, in which the rear wheels provide power; there also is four-wheel drive.) Among other things, front-wheel drive offers improved handling on slippery surfaces and provides more passenger room, because there is no ''hump'' going from the front engine to the rear wheels.

Fuel filter. A replaceable device installed in the fuel line that removes impurities before fuel reaches the carburetor.

Fuel injection. A system that ''injects'' the air/fuel mixture into each combustion chamber. It replaces a conventional carburetor and maximizes fuel economy. Because of its sophistication, it is more expensive to buy and maintain.

Fuel line. A small metal tube that connects the fuel tank to the carburetor or fuel injectors.

Fuel pump. It pumps fuel from the gas tank via the fuel line to the carburetor or fuel injectors.

Fuse. A protective device that self-destructs to shut down an electrical circuit during a malfunction. By doing so, it prevents serious damage to the rest of the electrical system. When a fuse breaks, you must replace it. If the new fuse breaks, it means there is something wrong that needs professional attention.

Handling. The ability of a car's suspension and tires

Glossary

to respond efficiently to movements of the steering wheel.

Hatchback. A body style with a lift-up door in the rear and no trunk.

Hydroplaning. A loss of control of the car, caused when a small sheet of water builds up between the road and a car's tires. This thin layer of water causes the car to lose contact with the road, resulting in a loss of steering and braking ability.

Idle. When the engine is running but isn't transmitting its power to the wheels, such as when waiting at a stop sign. A car's idle can be adjusted to the manufacturer's recommendations to maximize fuel efficiency.

Idler arm. Part of the steering linkage.

Independent rear suspension. A suspension system in which each rear wheel's movements are controlled individually, as opposed to having both rear wheels move in unison. This system contributes to good handling on rough or winding roads.

Jack. A portable device operated by a lever, screw, or other mechanical principle, used to raise the car to change a flat tire or perform other work.

Jumper cables. See **Booster cables.**

Leaf spring. A type of spring used in the suspension system.

Lug wrench. A wrench used to remove and install lug nuts, which connect the wheel to the axle or brake rotor.

Lugging. A shaking motion that usually occurs when the transmission gear is too high for the car's speed. You can eliminate lugging simply by shifting into a lower gear.

MacPherson struts. A type of suspension device in which the shock absorber, springs, and other components are combined into one unit. These devices contribute to better handling, but they are more expensive to repair or replace.

Manifold. The section between the carburetor and

the engine, containing one or more inlets (through which the air/fuel mixture enters the cylinders) and two or more outlets (through which exhaust gases leave the cylinders). The former is called an "intake manifold"; the latter is an "exhaust manifold."

Master cylinder. A container that stores brake fluid and transmits it through brake lines to the brakes.

Modulator. A small vacuum device that senses engine load to assure smooth shifting of transmission gears according to driving speed.

Muffler. A canister-like silencer that reduces the noise of the exhaust gases before they are released through the tailpipe.

Notchback. This popular car body style is essentially a fastback design with a section "notched" out of the roof line. The trunk is more distinct, providing a separate luggage compartment.

Odometer. A gauge on the dashboard that indicates how many miles the car has been driven. Under federal law, you are not allowed to tamper with this device; it must reflect the entire number of miles driven since the car came off the assembly line.

Oil filter. A can-shaped, replaceable filter that cleans the engine oil as it travels through the lubrication system.

Oil pump. This pumps the engine oil from the crankcase to lubricate the moving parts of the engine.

Overdrive. A gear added to a transmission to boost fuel economy at highway speeds. It permits the engine to run at a slightly slower speed without sacrificing performance. The result is that your engine must not work as hard and saves fuel as well as wear and tear. On manual-transmission cars, this gear often is called "fourth gear" or "fifth gear." It is built into the transmission system of some automatic-transmission cars.

PCV valve. It stands for "positive crankcase ventilation" and serves to pull harmful exhaust vapors out of the crankcase and burn them safely before they are released into the atmosphere.

Glossary

Piston. A can-shaped object that moves up and down inside each cylinder. As it moves, it compresses the air/fuel mixture to make it highly explosive. At the height of compression, a sparkplug ignites the mixture, resulting in "internal combustion."

Pitman arm. Part of the steering linkage.

Power brake booster. A device located between the brake pedal and the master cylinder that supplements your foot pressure to make braking easier.

Power steering pump. It pressurizes hydraulic power steering fluid to help you turn the front wheels more easily.

Quarter panel. The front or rear quarter section of a car's body. Each car has a right-front quarter panel, a right-rear quarter panel, a left-front quarter panel, and a left-rear quarter panel.

Rack-and-pinion steering. A steering system found on some cars that uses a "rack"—a gear-toothed tie rod—and a "pinion"—a gear mounted to the steering shaft. When you turn the steering wheel, the teeth of the rack mesh with the gear of the pinion, resulting in precise steering response.

Radiator. This maze of metal tubes cools the water/coolant mixture, which becomes very hot as it flows through the engine block. The radiator is attached to the engine block through radiator hoses.

Rear-wheel drive. See **Front-wheel drive.**

Rocker panel. The section of a car's body below the door opening. It usually runs from the front-wheel opening to the rear-wheel opening.

Rotor. This turns inside the distributor, making thousands of electrical contacts each minute, causing sparkplugs to fire in a precise sequence.

RPM. Revolutions per minute, a measurement of how fast the engine is turning, although not necessarily how fast the car is going. During one complete revolution, each cylinder goes through one air/fuel/sparkplug explosion.

Shock absorbers. Devices in the suspension system

that control the bouncing of the car as it turns and goes over bumps. They smooth out the ride and keep the wheels firmly on the road. There is one shock absorber for each wheel.

Solenoid. A device that connects the battery to the starter motor.

Sparkplug. This delivers an electrical spark to ignite the air/fuel mixture, resulting in the ''internal combustion'' that runs a car. Sparkplugs are connected to the rest of a car's electrical system via sparkplug wires.

Springs. Parts of the suspension system that cushion and absorb shocks and keep the car level on turns. There are various types of springs, including coil springs, leaf springs, and torsion bars.

Stabilizer bar. Also known as an ''anti-sway bar,'' this is mounted on the front and/or rear suspension. It allows the axle and both wheels to move up or down when going over bumps and dips, resulting in a smoother ride and better handling.

Starter motor. An electric motor that turns the flywheel, which, in turn, makes the engine ''turn over.''

Steering column. The section below the steering wheel that transmits your turning action from the steering wheel to the steering linkage. The column also holds the wires that control your horn, turn signals, and, on some automatic-transmission cars, the mechanism that sends the gear selection to the transmission.

Steering linkage. The connection between the steering column and the front wheels that makes the wheels change direction. The linkage includes a pitman arm and an idler arm.

Tachometer. A speedometer-like gauge that indicates how many revolutions per minute (RPM) the engine's crankshaft is turning.

Tailpipe. The last link in the exhaust system. It conducts exhaust gases from the muffler out into the atmosphere.

Glossary

Thermostat. A temperature-control device that helps prevent overheating.

Tie rod. Part of the linkage between the steering gear and the front wheels.

Toe-in. An adjustment to the front wheels that helps to keep the car going in a straight line.

Torque. The twisting power generated by the engine and transmitted to the driving wheels. This term also refers to the twisting force used to tighten nuts or other fasteners. Torque is expressed in ''pounds per square inch.''

Torsion bar. A type of spring used in the suspension system.

Transaxle. The combination of the transmission and the axle, generally found in front-wheel-drive cars.

Turbocharger. A pump-like device that recycles exhaust gases to boost an engine's power.

Universal joints (U-joints). These attach the driveshaft to the transmission on one end and to the differential on the other.

Voltage regulator. A device that monitors the amount of electricity the alternator sends to the battery. If it's not sending enough, you'll know from the red indicator light on your dashboard.

Water pump. It pumps water or antifreeze through the engine and back to the radiator.

Wheel. A circular rim and hub mounted to each axle. Tires are mounted on them.

Wheel alignment. Adjustments to the front wheels to ensure proper tire wear and steering performance. Types of adjustments include ''camber,'' ''caster,'' and ''toe-in.''

Wheel balancing. A technique in which small weights are added to the rim of a wheel to offset any imbalance.

Wheelbase. The distance from the center of a car's front wheel to the center of its rear wheel.

Index

Index

Index

tachometer, 151
tailgating, 124
tailpipe, 26-28, 138
temperature light, 118
test-driving a new car, 96-97
thermostat, 42-44
tie rod, 152
tilt steering wheel, 93, 94
tilt-up moon roof, 94
tinted glass, 94
tires and wheels, 15, 58-62, 134, 140
  adjustments, 62
  air pressure, 50, 129, 134, 140
  cleaning, 70
  tire wear, 52, 56, 58-62, 140
title application, 98-99
toe-in adjustment, 62
tools, 65-66, 118
torque, 152
torsion bars, 54
touch-ups, paint, 68
trade-ins, 97
transaxle, 152
transmission system, 15, 30-34, 134, 139
  automatic vs. manual, 93
trim, 71
troubleshooting guide, 132-135
tune-ups, 21, 24, 78, 129
turbocharger, 152
"two-second rule," 124

universal joints, 30-33
used cars, 102-104

vapor lock, 113
vinyl roofs, 94
  cleaning, 72
vinyl trim, 71
vinyl upholstery, 67
voltage regulator, 19, 20

warning lights, dashboard, 118
washing, 69
water jackets, 42-43
water pump, 42-44, 139
waxing, 70-72
WD-40, 66
weather-stripping, 71
wheel see also tires and wheels
  alignment, 50, 62, 140
  balancing, 50, 62
  cylinder, 46-47, 49
wheel, steering, see steering wheel
wheelbase, 152
windows, cleaning, 72
windshield washer, 20, 138
windshield wipers, 20, 71, 116, 138
wire wheel covers, 94
wrenches, 65-66

Index

Important Information

Car Make _____ Model _____

Body Style _____ Year _____

Vehicle Identification Number _____

Key Serial Numbers:

_____
Ignition   Door   Trunk

Insurance Agent:

_____
Company   Phone   Policy Number

Mechanic:

_____
Name   Phone

Auto Club:

_____
Phone   Membership Number